THE
EGYPTIAN ORIGINS
OF
KING DAVID
AND THE
TEMPLE *of* SOLOMON

"No one since Sigmund Freud has done more to show the connection between ancient Egypt's Amarna period and the biblical stories of Joseph, Moses, and the Exodus. Ahmed Osman now provides compelling new evidence showing the true roots behind the establishment of the kingdom of Israel and the building of the Temple of Solomon."

ANDREW COLLINS, AUTHOR OF
THE CYGNUS KEY AND *GÖBEKLI TEPE:*
GENESIS OF THE GODS

"Ahmed Osman has discovered an intriguing back door into biblical history. Walking the tightrope between skeptical archaeologists and true believers of the Bible, the author asks a compelling question: Did Hebrew scribes attribute the military victories of an Egyptian pharaoh to David, the famous slayer of Goliath?"

RAND AND ROSE FLEM-ATH, AUTHORS OF
THE MURDER OF MOSES: HOW AN EGYPTIAN MAGICIAN
ASSASSINATED MOSES, STOLE HIS IDENTITY,
AND HIJACKED THE EXODUS

THE
EGYPTIAN ORIGINS
OF
KING DAVID
AND THE
TEMPLE *of* SOLOMON

AHMED OSMAN

Bear & Company
Rochester, Vermont

Bear & Company
One Park Street
Rochester, Vermont 05767
www.BearandCompanyBooks.com

Text stock is SFI certified

Bear & Company is a division of Inner Traditions International

Library of Congress Cataloging-in-Publication Data

Names: Osman, Ahmed, 1934- author.
Title: The Egyptian origins of King David and the Temple of Solomon / Ahmed Osman.
Description: Rochester, Vermont : Bear & Company, [2019] | Includes bibliographical references and index.
Identifiers: LCCN 2018030765 (print) | LCCN 2018032391 (ebook) | ISBN 9781591433019 (paperback) | ISBN 9781591433026 (ebook)
Subjects: LCSH: David, King of Israel. | Temple of Jerusalem (Jerusalem) | Jews—History—1200-953 B.C. | Jews—Civilization—Egyptian influences. | Egypt—History—To 332 B.C. | BISAC: BODY, MIND & SPIRIT / Mythical Civilizations. | RELIGION / Biblical Criticism & Interpretation / Old Testament. | HISTORY / Civilization.
Classification: LCC BS580.D3 O86 2019 (print) | LCC BS580.D3 (ebook) | DDC 222/.4092—dc23
LC record available at https://lccn.loc.gov/2018030765

Printed and bound in the United States by Lake Book Manufacturing, Inc. The text stock is SFI certified. The Sustainable Forestry Initiative® program promotes sustainable forest management.

10 9 8 7 6 5 4 3 2 1

Text design by Virgina Scott Bowman and layout by Debbie Glogover
This book was typeset in Garamond Premier Pro with Librum and Gill Sans MT Pro used for display fonts

To send correspondence to the author of this book, mail a first-class letter to the author c/o Inner Traditions • Bear & Company, One Park Street, Rochester, VT 05767, and we will forward the communication.

To the followers of Hermes Trismegistus—
those people, in different parts of the world,
who never forgot the wisdom of ancient Egypt.

My gratitude to Kayla Toher and Richard Smoley for their help in preparing the manuscript for publication.

Israel is the illegitimate son of Egypt,
Who challenges his father to accept him.

Contents

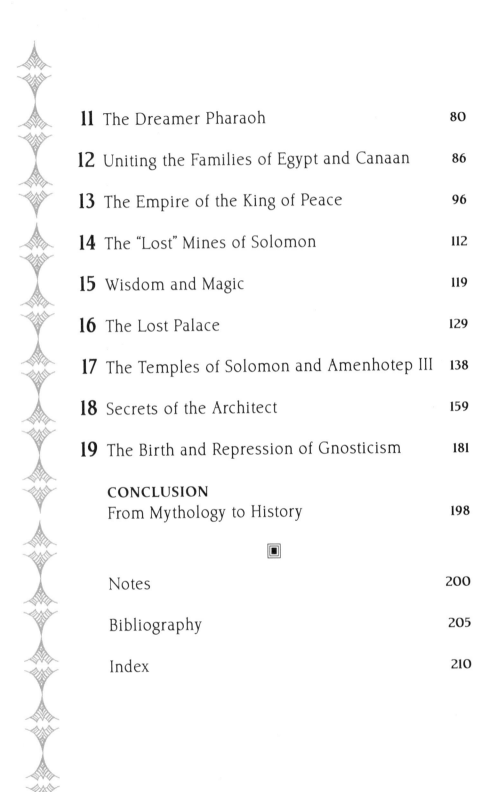

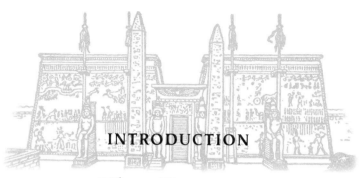

The History
behind the Bible

THE BIBLE IS A BOOK OF RELIGIOUS FAITH that includes many miraculous events and supernatural characters, an account of the creation of the universe, Adam and Eve, and the Flood—all of which could be understood symbolically. But the Old Testament also mentions ordinary people living within an allegedly historical framework, such as Abraham, Jacob, Joseph, Moses, David, and Solomon.

In modern times, historians and archaeologists have found no evidence to confirm the biblical accounts of these characters and their stories. As a result, some have tried to force the evidence to agree with the biblical account; others have completely denied the historicity of the Bible stories, regarding the accounts of Moses, David, and Solomon as fiction.

I do not agree with either of these views. I believe that the core of the biblical account does describe historical characters and events. But the biblical editors, who wrote the stories, placed them, chronologically and geographically, in the wrong place.

The script originally used to write Hebrew only emerged sometime in the tenth century BCE, as a development of the Phoenician script, with which it is more or less identical. Consequently, the first books of the Bible could only have been written after this date, more than three centuries after the time of Moses, who supposedly lived in the fourteenth and thirteenth centuries BCE. One then wonders: if the Hebrew script had not yet been developed in Moses's time, which script did God use to write the Ten Commandments?

After centuries of oral transmission, the biblical writers had available to them many different traditions, as well as written historical information, from neighboring countries such as Babylonia, Syria, and Egypt. To judge by the way they composed their stories, it seems that the scribes must have placed some accounts either in the wrong chronological time or in the wrong geographical location. In my view, this is the main reason why historians and archaeologists have failed to find verifying evidence. However, when we place the biblical stories into their correct historical settings, we do find confirmation.

As we shall see in this book, I believe that evidence for the principal biblical stories can be found not in Canaan but in Egypt, during the Eighteenth Dynasty, in the fifteenth and fourteenth centuries BCE. Although the Israelites were originally only one of many historically unknown Hebrew tribes, they became part of recorded history when they intermarried with the pharaonic house of Egypt.

1

The Man of God

KING DAVID, ONE OF THE MOST FASCINATING CHARACTERS in the Bible, was a courageous and cunning man, a complex figure larger than life. Looked upon as "a man after God's own heart," David is believed to have been able to understand the mind of the divine being. He is thought to have lived in the tenth century BCE, to have reigned as king of Israel for forty years, and to have died at the age of seventy.

David was a shepherd, a descendant of Judah, one of Israel's twelve sons. He lived in Bethlehem before he was anointed by the prophet Samuel to be the king of Israel. David is known for his diverse skills as a warrior and is said to have established a great empire extending between the river Euphrates in northern Syria and the river Nile in Egypt. He is also known to have been a musician and a poet, and seventy-three of the 150 Psalms in the Bible are attributed to him. David is also regarded by Islam as a prophet and messenger of God who received the divine revelation of the Psalms. We can see the beauty of his soul when we read his Psalms:

> The LORD is my shepherd, I lack nothing. He makes me lie down
> in green pastures, he leads me beside quiet waters, he refreshes my
> soul. (Psalm 23:1–2)

David is promised by God that even after his death, his descendants will continue to rule his great empire. His bloodline will become the only legitimate royal bloodline in Jewish history. As the Bible says: "The word of the LORD came to Nathan [the prophet], Go and tell my servant David, . . . When your days are fulfilled and you rest with your ancestors, I will raise up your offspring after you, your own flesh and blood, and I will establish his kingdom. He is the one who will build a house for my Name, and I will establish the throne of his kingdom forever. I will be his father, and he shall be my son" (2 Samuel 7:4–5; 12–14).

So, like the Egyptian pharaohs, David regarded himself as a son of God: "[The LORD] said to me, You are my son; today I have become your father" (Psalm 2:7). Ultimately, at the end of history, the Messiah will come from the line of David. We find several verses in the Bible relating to the future of the Davidic messiah: "The days are coming, declares the LORD, when I will raise up for David a righteous Branch, a King who will reign wisely and do what is just and right in the land" (Jeremiah 23:5). While the Jews are still waiting for their messiah, Christians believe that this prophecy was fulfilled in Jesus Christ.

After their Exodus from Egypt and their settlement in the Promised Land, the Israelites formed a loose confederation under the leadership of judges. At the time of the prophet Samuel, the twelfth and last of these judges, the Israelites came under attack from the Philistines, whose five fortified cities, Ashdod, Gaza, Ashkelon, Gath, and Ekron, were on the southeastern shore of the Mediterranean Sea, between modern-day Tel Aviv and the Gaza Strip. After the Israelites were defeated by the Philistines, the elders thought to bring the Ark of the Covenant from Shiloh (the modern Khirbet Seilun in Samaria) into their camp to help them in their fight. This is supposed to have been the Ark of the Covenant that Moses had placed in the Holy of Holies in the Tabernacle he built in the wilderness after the Exodus, and in which he placed the Ten Commandments. Nevertheless, not only were the Israelites defeated again in battle, but the Philistines took the ark from them. At that point the people of Israel demanded to have a king to rule over them, like other nations, so they could face the threat of the Philistines. Under direction from God, Samuel anointed Saul, son of Kish the Benjaminite, as the first king over Israel, from his town, Gibeah, north of Jerusalem.

When King Saul needed someone to play the harp for him, he sent his messengers to Jesse of Judah in Bethlehem, asking for David, his youngest son, to come and see him. At the time, David was only a lad of about fifteen who loved music and who looked after his father's sheep in the field. When Saul met David, he was pleased with him and kept him in his service as a musician.

As Saul and the Israelites came to the western edge of the Judah hills, facing the Philistines in the Valley of Elah, Goliath, the Philistine giant of Gath, challenged them to send out their champion so that the outcome could be decided in single combat. None of the Israelites dared to come forth, but when young David, who was bringing food to his elder brothers in the army, heard that Goliath had defied the armies of God, he amazed everybody by offering to confront the nine-foot-tall, bronze-armored Philistine giant. With God's help, the challenge became easy for David. Invoking God's name, he hurled a stone from his sling, which hit Goliath in the center of his forehead. Goliath fell on his face to the ground, and David quickly cut off his head. Seeing the fate of their great giant, the Philistines abandoned fighting and fled from the battlefield.

Saul admired the boy's courage and appointed David as commander of his men. Soon, however, David became the people's hero, and the king became jealous of him. Hoping that he might perish in fighting, Saul offered him the hand of his daughter, Michal, in exchange for the foreskins of a hundred Philistines as her bride-price. David slew two hundred Philistines and brought their foreskins to the king. Saul's jealousy of David increased even more, and he decided to kill him. When he learned of the king's plan, David fled from Saul with six hundred of his supporters and joined the service of Achish, the Philistine king of Gath, home of the dead Goliath (1 Sam 21:10).

After one year and four months in Gath, fighting broke out again between the Israelites and the Philistines, which resulted in the death of Saul and three of his sons. Hearing about Saul's death, David left Gath and went with his six hundred men to Hebron in the territory of Judah, where the people anointed him as their king. David was thirty years of age when he began his reign.

At the same time, Saul's son Ishbosheth was proclaimed king over Israel. Soon after, war broke out between Judah and Israel and only came to an end when Ishbosheth was killed by two of his captains. David united the two kingdoms and ruled over all the tribes of Israel, and then he conquered the fortress of Jerusalem, which was inhabited by a Canaanite tribe called the Jebusites.

Having conquered Jerusalem, David decided to build his house there, and Hiram, king of Tyre in Phoenicia, sent cedar trees, carpenters, and masons to build David's fort, called the City of David. David then gathered together thirty thousand men of Israel and went to Gibeah (where the ark had been kept after being recovered from the Philistines) to bring the Ark of the Lord to Jerusalem. There he placed it in a tabernacle on Mount Moriah, north of the city.

Having established his capital in Jerusalem, David began fighting wars against Israel's neighbors. He was able to subdue the Philistine cities and conquer the remaining Canaanite city-states. He defeated the nations east of the river Jordan: the Moabites, the Edomites, and the Ammonites, as well as the Arameans of Syria. He also defeated Hadadezer, king of Zobah (in southern Syria), "as he went to recover his border at the river Euphrates" (2 Samuel 8:3, King James Version). He took from them a thousand chariots, seven hundred horsemen, and twenty thousand foot soldiers. He also put garrisons in Edom, southeast of Judah. Thus, according to the biblical account, David's empire extended between the river Euphrates in northern Syria to the northern Sinai in Egypt, including Syria, Canaan, and the territory east of the Jordan. In order to administer this large empire, David established civil and military administrations and divided the empire into twelve districts, each with its own civil, military, and religious institutions. He also put military garrisons in Syria.

David, the mighty king who ruled a great empire, was courageous on the battlefield, a passionate poet and lover, and a man of God, yet he had his own personal weakness—a destructive passion.

During the second year of his siege of Rabbah, east of the river Jordan, David stayed in Jerusalem. He arose one evening from his bed and from the roof of his palace saw a beautiful woman bathing. David learned that her name was Bathsheba and that she was the wife of Uriah the Hittite. As her husband was one of his men fighting at Rabbah, David sent messengers to bring Bathsheba to him, and he slept with her.

When Bathsheba informed him that she was pregnant, David, in an attempt to conceal his relations with the woman, recalled Uriah from the battlefront and encouraged him to go home and sleep with his wife. But Uriah, feeling it was not right to go to his house while the rest of the army was still in the fields, slept among David's servants instead.

When his plan failed, David ordered Uriah to be placed in the forefront of the battle so he would be killed. David then married Bathsheba, who became the mother of Solomon, the most important of his sons, who followed him on the throne.

We can see another contrast in David's character in his confrontation with his son Absalom. As a young lad of fifteen, David faced Goliath, the armored Philistine giant, but as a mighty conqueror who established a large empire, he was afraid to face his son Absalom when he decided to overthrow his father and rule in his stead.

Absalom became upset when his sister, Tamar, was raped by their half brother, Amnon. Absalom decided to leave Jerusalem and go to Hebron, where he declared himself king with the support of all Israel and Judah. When he learned that his son was coming back to take power in Jerusalem, David fled from the city with his six hundred men, who followed him from Gath, seeking refuge east of the Jordan. So Absalom took over Jerusalem, the City of David, without any challenge and ruled David's empire. Absalom then crossed the Jordan with his army in pursuit of his father, but when the two sides confronted each other in a final battle, Absalom's army was defeated and Absalom himself was killed.

David went back to Jerusalem and resumed his reign over the empire until he was seventy years old. While David was still alive, Adonijah, his eldest surviving son, conspired to declare himself king. Adonijah was only stopped when Bathsheba persuaded David to appoint her son, Solomon, as his successor instead.

According to the Bible, King Solomon inherited his father's great empire, extending from the Euphrates in the north to the Sinai in the south: "Solomon ruled over all kingdoms from the Euphrates River to the land of the Philistines, as far as the border of Egypt. These countries brought tribute and were Solomon's subjects all his life" (1 Kings 4:21). Solomon also had a mighty army including two thousand horses with horsemen and fourteen hundred war chariots. But this empire completely disappeared after Solomon's death. And despite the widespread belief in the greatness of David and his empire, no historical or archaeological evidence has been found to confirm this story.

Were King David and his great empire just a fantasy, a fiction created by biblical scribes? Or was it a real historical story that had been mixed up by the scribes, who relied on different accounts from separate sources, causing the apparent contradictions in his character?

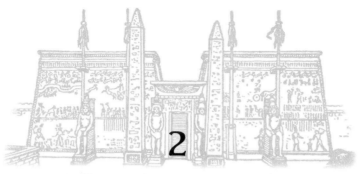

2

The Two Davids

THE BIBLICAL ACCOUNT OF DAVID presents him as a figure with many contradictions, which has suggested to modern scholars that his story came from more than one source. According to Israeli biblical scholar Moshe Garsiel, "The studies of the development of the story cycles created the impression that the book of Samuel is a product of the combination of sequential story cycles."[1]

That is why twentieth-century biblical scholars have characterized David in two contradictory ways: one, as a pious shepherd who rises to become the king of Israel; the other, as a cunning usurper who murders and schemes his way to a throne that is not rightfully his. The story of David begins with him being chosen by God, anointed by Samuel (1 Samuel 16:13), and hired as a court musician for King Saul (1 Samuel 16:17–23). Later, after David killed Goliath and returned from his successful battle with the Philistines, people loved him and women came from all the towns of Israel dancing and singing: "Saul has slain his thousands, and David his tens of thousands" (1 Samuel 18:7; compare with verse 21:12). It was then that King Saul became worried of David's intentions, suspecting that he was trying to usurp the throne, and tried to kill him. However, David escaped by going to the Philistines, enemies of Israel, and assembled an army with the aim of fighting Saul. The conflict ended when both

Saul and his son were killed in battle against the Philistines.

It was then that Abner, Saul's army commander, brought Ishbosheth, Saul's other son, and made him king of Israel (2 Samuel. 2:8–9). David, at the same time, went to Hebron, where he was anointed as king of Judah, and war between the two kings started (2 Samuel 3:1) Their war came to an end only with the assassination of Ishbosheth, which allowed David to unite Judah and Israel and move to Jerusalem.

Accordingly, various theories have been suggested regarding David's story as it appears in 1 and 2 Samuel. Julius Wellhausen, the prominent German biblical scholar, believed that the David story had two interwoven parallel sources, which were combined to make up most of the books of Samuel. He argued that the first and earlier main source was more realistic, while the second main source contained additional schematic and theological components.

A second attempt to explain the contradictions in the story of David was presented by the fragments theory. According to this theory, in their first stages, the books of 1 and 2 Samuel were a collection of fragmentary pieces of information, such as oral traditions, local sagas, and archival documents. Moreover, the scribes who put together the final product were primarily interested in David *not* as a historical figure but as a religious model.

The next stage in examining David's story came as a result of modern archaeological excavation in the Middle East. Since the mid-nineteenth century, thousands of ancient documents from different sites have been unearthed, providing information about the history, politics, religion, laws, customs, and almost every other aspect of life in the ancient world. At the top of their list, archaeologists excavating Syria and Palestine (ancient Canaan) looked for evidence to support the existence of David's empire in the tenth century BCE, as described in the Bible. In addition to David's house in Jerusalem, archaeologists sought artifacts related to Solomon, who is said to have conducted a great deal of building activity both in Jerusalem and in other parts of the empire. But no single piece of evidence has been found anywhere relating to the empire of David and Solomon. Not one goblet, not one brick, has ever been found to indicate that such an empire existed.

Moshe Garsiel comments: "The Land of Israel has been the object of intensive archaeological research since the late nineteenth century. In terms of settlements and archaeological finding in Jerusalem, the Judean Region, and other regions of the country are rather scanty. Some scholars believe that the urban infrastructure for a polity such as the great kingdom and Solomon as depicted in the books of Samuel and Kings was completely lacking."[2]

Furthermore, if David and Solomon ruled a large empire during the tenth century BCE, archaeologists could expect to find their names mentioned in the diplomatic correspondence of other nations of the day, such as Egypt and Mesopotamia; yet once again the record is silent.

We would expect that a famous king like David would have left some archaeological remains of his existence, or that he would be mentioned in the records of the ancient countries he conquered. However, no single piece of evidence has come to show that he ever existed; the Bible is our only source of information about David and his empire. The absence of outside evidence has persuaded modern scholars to take a critical stand against the biblical story, and some of them have even denied the existence of King David.

King David and King Solomon in all his splendour, never existed, a 15-year study of archaeological evidence has concluded.

The study—by Professor Thomas Thompson, one of the world's foremost authorities of biblical archaeology—says that the first 10 books of the Old Testament are almost certainly fiction, written between 500 and 1,500 years after the events they purport to describe.

Thompson's claims, outlined in a new book, *The Early History of the Israelite People,* are being taken seriously by scholars. The

British Museum's leading expert on the archaeology of the Holy Land, Jonathan Tubb, said last week: "Professor Thompson may well be right in many of his arguments. His book is a work of tremendous scholarship."[3]

As Philip R. Davies, a prominent Welsh scholar, admitted, "I am not the only scholar who suspects that the figure of King David is about as historical as King Arthur."[4]

Even otherwise, the story of a tribal chief's founding of an empire stretching from the Nile to the Euphrates has posed problems for scholars. It does not equate with the fact that he is known to have had an army of just six hundred men. Furthermore, no such empire is known to have been created between the time of Tuthmosis III in the fifteenth century BCE and the second half of the sixth century BCE, when Cyrus of Persia conquered both Mesopotamia and Egypt. Nowadays the main argument among scholars is between those who hold that David was a local chieftain living in Judea south of Jerusalem, whose authority extended only a few miles in any direction, and those who completely deny his existence.

The task of identifying the historical David is complicated by the fact that the Old Testament provides us with two contrasting characters who cannot have been the same person. One is a mighty warrior who has lost his northern borders at the Euphrates and goes out fighting to regain his land. In the process, he recovers a large empire, including the whole land of Canaan down to the Egyptian border, the lands east of the Jordan, and all of the Syrian territory east of the Euphrates. He has a great army with thousands of chariots and horsemen, unlike the other David, who has only six hundred followers.

Nevertheless, the biblical narrative indicates that the original story was related to the tribal David only, and that the account of King David's empire was added to it in order to exalt him from a tribal chief to a mighty king. To make this contradiction believable, the narrator(s) used an additional account, introducing the story of David's confrontation with Goliath. Then again, to allow for Solomon to be his successor, the biblical scribe used yet another source, describing the story of David's passion with a married woman, Bathsheba.

3

The Evidence
of Archaeology

FOR MORE THAN TWO THOUSAND YEARS, when our knowledge
of ancient history was derived only from the Bible, the Qur'an, and
classical writers, the story of King David was taken to represent
historical reality. During this period, many works of art and literature represented David as a hero who, starting as a young shepherd, became a mighty king, ruling a great empire between the
Nile and the Euphrates in the tenth century BCE. With the start
of archaeological excavation in the Holy Land in the middle of the
nineteenth century, however, the situation changed dramatically, as
the information uncovered has given a completely different picture
about him.

When we examine David's story, we realize that in his time the
conflict between the Israelites and the Philistines had erupted into
continuous fighting. We also realize that while the Israelites, following their Exodus from Egypt, were entering Canaan from the east, the
Philistines were arriving from the sea at the Mediterranean coast on
the west. Only after establishing themselves in coastal cities did the
Philistines decide to extend their domination to the east.

THE ISRAELITES' ENTRY
INTO THE PROMISED LAND

The Old Testament, again, provides us with two contradictory accounts of the arrival of the Israelites in the Promised Land of Canaan. The version that has gained most popular acceptance is that Canaan was conquered by Joshua, Moses's successor, in a swift military campaign during the latter part of the thirteenth century BCE. On the other hand, according to the book of Judges, the Israelites' occupation was a fragmentary process involving individual tribes in various local conflicts and taking place over a long period of time. This latter view has been confirmed by modern archaeology.

Following the Exodus, the Israelites first dwelt for a long time in the area of Mount Seir in Edom, stretching between the Dead Sea and the Gulf of Aqaba in the south. Memory of those days can be seen in the Song of Deborah: "When you, LORD, went out from Seir, when you marched from the land of Edom, the earth shook, the heavens poured, the clouds poured down water. The mountains quaked before the LORD, the One of Sinai, before the LORD, the God of Israel" (Judges 5:4–5).

This indicates that during the second decade of the thirteenth century BCE, the Israelites—evidently still seminomadic—had left Egypt but were located in the area of Mount Seir in Edom, between the south end of the Dead Sea and Elath, at the head of the Gulf of Aqaba. It was only when Egypt had lost control over Canaan in the second half of the twelfth century BCE that the Israelites started to infiltrate the land from Dan (in upper Galilee, near the source of the river Jordan) in the north to Beersheba in the Negev Desert to the south, where archaeological excavation has shown evidence of new settlement during the twelfth century BCE. At that time the Israelites were still living in the ruins of ancient cities or among other Canaanite inhabitants.

The land of Canaan at the time of the Israelites'
entry into the Holy Land, ca. 1200 BCE

THE ARRIVAL OF THE PHILISTINES

The land of Canaan remained firmly under Egyptian control when Ramses III (ca. 1182–1151 BCE), the second ruler of Egypt's Twentieth Dynasty, came to the throne. A papyrus found in Thebes—known as the Papyrus Harris and now in the British Museum—relates that at this comparatively late date, Ramses III built a temple of Amun in the land of Canaan, and the "foreigners of Retenu come to it, bearing their tributes before it." Furthermore, an ivory pen case found at the Canaanite city of Megiddo and belonging to an Egyptian envoy to foreign countries bears the name of Ramses III.[1]

When the reign of Ramses III came to an end, Egypt lost control over Canaan. The main reason for Egypt's loss was the mass invasion of Canaan by the "peoples of the sea." This invasion had begun around 1174 BCE, year 8 of Ramses III (about the same time that, according to Greek tradition, the Trojan War was taking place). The invaders' story is recorded in the best-preserved inscriptions and reliefs on the walls of Ramses III's funerary temple in western Thebes. The reliefs depict people who were seeking permanent settlement, with whole families on the move, traveling by oxcart with women, children, and household possessions: "Their confederation consisted of Peleset, Tjekker, Shklesh, Danu and Weshesh, united lands."[2]

The invading Peleset are recognized as the Philistines, who later gave their name to the land of Canaan—Palestine. The Hittite empire of Asia Minor, as well as northern Syria, was also swept away by the invaders, and the Hittite capital, Hattushash, was burned to the ground. Although Ramses III was able to defeat the Sea Peoples when they attacked Egypt, archaeological evidence shows that they had been settled in the coastal area of Canaan before the end of his reign in the mid-twelfth century BCE. The archaeological evidence consists of a class of painted Mycenaean pottery that has been found in southwest Canaan, dating from the first half of the twelfth century BCE.

Although this pottery follows the long-established Mycenaean Greek tradition in color, shape, and painted motifs, chemical and physical analyses indicate that it was made locally. This suggests that the Sea Peoples' original homeland was in the Aegean or western Asia Minor, which agrees with the Bible in naming the original homeland of the Philistines as "Caphtor" in Crete (Amos 9:7; Jeremiah 47:4).

According to the British archaeologist Kathleen Kenyon:

> It was in the second half of the twelfth century BCE that the Philistines really established themselves by building older towns and founding new ones, often no doubt in close association with the Canaanite population they now ruled. Ashdod was remodelled to a new layout and strongly fortified. At Tel Qasile, in the northern suburbs of modern Tel Aviv on the Yarkon river, a new maritime settlement was established. Elsewhere there is a varied archaeological record of urban recession, as at Aphek and Lachish, or of richly equipped cemeteries, as at Azor, where the contemporary settlement remains unknown.[3]

The story of David starts when the Philistines had already established their city-states in southwestern Canaan and were attempting to expand east toward the Dead Sea and the river Jordan. At the same time the Israelites too were trying to establish themselves in the area. Thus conflict between these two new arrivals became the main preoccupation both of Saul and of the tribal David.

THE CAPTURE OF JERUSALEM

According to the Bible, after the death of Saul, when David became king of the united Israelite tribes, he began his wars outside the land of Israel. His first campaign after becoming sole ruler over the Israelites is described in 2 Samuel:

The king and his men marched to Jerusalem to attack the Jebusites, who lived there. The Jebusites said to David, "You will not get in here." . . . Nevertheless, David captured the fortress of Zion—which is the City of David. On that day David had said, "Anyone who conquers the Jebusites will have to use the water shaft." . . . David then took up residence in the fortress and called it the City of David. He built up the area around it, from the terraces inward. . . . Now Hiram king of Tyre sent envoys to David, along with cedar logs and carpenters and stonemasons, and they built a palace for David. (2 Samuel 5:6–11)

The reference to "the king and his men" indicates that it was the ruler and his bodyguard, not his entire army, who were involved. As for the "water shaft" by which they obtained entry to the fortress, this is thought to have been a shaft dug to ensure supplies of water from a spring known as the Gihon—the Christian Virgin Fountain—that lay in the valley some 325 meters below Jerusalem.

Israel Finkelstein, professor of archaeology at Tel Aviv University, gives an account of modern excavation work in Jerusalem:

As archaeological research in Jerusalem continued and expanded, it became clear that the best location for finding archaeological remains from the time of David and Solomon was not on the Temple Mount or among the close-packed buildings within the walled Ottoman city, but on a narrow, steep ridge that extended South of the Temple Mount, beyond the walls. This area was identified as . . . the "Ophel," or the "City of David" mentioned repeatedly in the biblical text. Indeed, this is the tell, or ancient mound, containing layers of accumulation and structures from Bronze and Iron Age Jerusalem. This ridge became the scene of large-scale excavations throughout the twentieth century.

The ancient remains uncovered here have always been quite

fragmentary. Each of the major excavators in this part of Jerusalem . . . argued that because of the steepness of the slope and destructive force of continuous erosion, the full extent of the Davidic city had been lost. Still, here and there among the various excavation areas, they found deposits of pottery or isolated architectural elements that they connected to the time of David, in the tenth century BCE. . . . However, these claims were based on a kind of circular reasoning. Beginning with the assumption that the biblical narratives were reliable historical sources, the researchers identified these ruins as features mentioned in the Bible. And they used the hypothetical identifications as archaeological "proof" that the biblical descriptions were true.[4]

Finkelstein's conclusion is supported by archaeologist Philip R. Davies: "Jerusalem, and despite extensive excavation, had not yield [*sic*] the kind of evidence that would suggest the capital of a powerful kingdom at this time. There is plenty of pottery from earlier and later periods, but not much for Iron I or IIa."[5] (Iron Age I and IIa correspond to 1200–700 BCE.)

The Bible tells us that Hiram, king of Tyre, sent his men to David in Jerusalem to build him a house. Although modern archaeologists have tried their best to find David's house in Jerusalem, they have found no indication of it. It is true that in 2005 Eilat Mazar, an Israeli archaeologist, announced that she had unearthed David's palace. She identified it as a large stone structure south of the Old City of Jerusalem, which she dated to his time in the tenth century BCE.

However, "a senior Israeli archaeologist rejected Mazar's claim: 'She knew what she was doing,' says fellow archaeologist David Ilan of the Hebrew Union College. 'She waded into the fray purposefully, wanting to make a statement.' Ilan himself doubts that Mazar has found King David's palace. 'My gut tells me this is an eighth- or ninth-century building,' he says, constructed a hundred years or more after Solomon died in 930 BCE."[6]

Critics also question Mazar's motives. Robert Draper writes in *National Geographic* magazine:

They note that her excavation work was underwritten by two organizations—the City of David Foundation and the Shalem Center, [both organizations that are] dedicated to the assertion of Israel's territorial rights. And they scoff at Mazar's allegiance to the antiquated methods of her archaeological forebears, such as her grandfather, who unapologetically worked with a trowel in one hand and a Bible in the other.

The once common practice of using the Bible as an archaeological guide has been widely contested as an unscientific case of circular reasoning—and with particular relish by Tel Aviv University's contrarian-in-residence Israel Finkelstein, who has made a career out of merrily demolishing such assumptions. He . . . says that the weight of archaeological evidence in and around Israel suggests that the dates posited by biblical scholars are a century off. The "Solomonic" buildings excavated by biblical archaeologists over the past several decades at Hazor, Gezer, and Megiddo were not constructed in David and Solomon's time. . . .

During David's time, as Finkelstein casts it, Jerusalem was little more than a "hill-county village," David himself a ragged upstart akin to Pancho Villa, and his legion of followers more like "500 people with sticks in their hands shouting and cursing and spitting—not the stuff of great armies of chariots described in the text."[7]

WARS OF EMPIRE

According to the biblical account, David, having established his residence in Jerusalem, went out to conquer the rest of Canaan, including the Philistine cities. We are told that as soon as the Philistines heard of David's appointment as king of Israel, they set out to do battle with him and "spread out in the valley of Rephaim" to the northwest of Bethlehem. This resulted in two encounters, in the second of which David "struck down the Philistines all the way from Gibeon to Gezer," one of the coastal cities north of Ashdod (2 Samuel 5:18–25).

Following this victory, David is reported to have conquered Moab on the east side of the Dead Sea (2 Samuel 8:2) and Zobah in northern Syria (2 Samuel 8:3), and to have "gat him a name" (erected a stele) by the Euphrates, in southern Asia Minor. He also put garrisons in Damascus and conquered Edom in south Canaan (2 Samuel 8:13), bordering the Egyptian Sinai, as well as defeated the Ammonites and conquered their city, Rabbah (modern Amman in Jordan; 2 Samuel 11:1).

After excavating Jerusalem, scholarly attention shifted to the sites of three important ancient cities—Megiddo, Hazor, and Gezer—that are specifically mentioned in the Bible in connection with King Solomon's ambitious building activities (1 Kings 9:15).

Megiddo, also known as Tell el-Mutesellim, was the first of these three cities to become the scene of intensive archaeological excavations. It commanded the "Way of the Sea," which branched off the main coastal "Way of the Land" of the Philistines, which started at Zarw, the border city of Egypt in northern Sinai, and led to upper Galilee and northern Syria. Its strategic situation made it important for both trade and military purposes. Megiddo is said to have been destroyed by the Israelites and rebuilt by Solomon.

Since the start of the last century, the excavations carried out at Megiddo at various times have been the most extensive in Palestine's history. In the 1920s, in the course of excavations by the Oriental Institute of the University of Chicago, remains were found that were identified as representing the time of Solomon. Later, Yigael Yadin, the Israeli archaeologist and military general, confirmed that Megiddo was the Canaanite city burned by King David.

Nevertheless, Philip R. Davies concluded that "the cause of the burning of this city (Megiddo) must be attributed to something or someone else (other than David). The other major candidate is the Egyptian pharaoh Sheshonq, whom 1 Kings 11:40 dates to the reign of Solomon. Sheshonq left a stele in Egypt on which he claimed to have conquered 180 places in Palestine, and . . . 1 Kings 14:25 says that he did come against the city, and the traditional view therefore concluded that Sheshonq brought an end to Solomon's empire."[8]

Davies's conclusion is supported by the Bible, which says that Pharaoh Shishak (Sheshonq) campaigned in Israel and Judah right after the death of King Solomon; furthermore, Solomon's city at Megiddo was destroyed in an intense conflagration, and a stele of Sheshonq was found at the site. From that point on, the entire construct of the history and material culture of the Solomonic state rested on these finds.

Hazor, the second city in the list, is the largest ancient mound in Israel, located north of the Sea of Galilee, with layers of occupation stretching back to the Early Bronze Age. Gezer, the third city mentioned, is a large site strategically located in the Valley of Aijalon, guarding the road from the coast to Jerusalem. Archaeological evidence shows that Hazor, Gezer, and the other Canaanite cities were not destroyed by the Israelites in the tenth century BCE but had been destroyed two centuries earlier by the Philistines. The destruction of these cities "occurred at the same time as the destruction of Hazor and other Syrian and Canaanite cities by the Philistines, the 'people of the Sea.'"[9]

Rabbah, present-day Amman, is the capital of the Hashemite kingdom of Jordan. Excavation work there after the Second World War revealed remains including a temple and the residue of an ancient wall dating from the ninth century BCE, a century later than the time of David. Most of the other buildings and tombs unearthed belonged to the period between the ninth century BCE and Roman times. Therefore archaeology has not offered any evidence to justify the biblical claim that David conquered Rabbah in the first half of the tenth century BCE. No walls dating from this period have been found, and it would seem to have been a minor settlement then.

As for Zobah, it has been identified as Qadesh, once a northern Syrian stronghold on the river Orontes. The archaeological evidence here again shows no evidence of destruction at the time of David. Moreover, the city was unfortified—thus not needing a siege to subdue it—in the first half of the tenth century BCE.

The result of excavation work in the sites mentioned in the Bible as being conquered by David showed no evidence to support this account. Philip Davies writes, "Neither David nor Solomon exists outside the biblical texts, and it is not at all clear that without the literary portrait any archaeologist would be able to infer such figures. That a single kingdom in central Palestine can be inferred at this time is unlikely, and the existence of a kingdom of the biblical dimensions is definitely out of the question."[10]

Modern excavation work has challenged the historical reliability of the Bible. In recent years, scholars have been locked in a battle over the historicity of the biblical account of David in the Bible. The debate started in the 1990s, when Finkelstein challenged the traditional idea of a great United Monarchy of Israel, established in the course of the military exploits of King David and stabilized in the days of his son Solomon, who ruled a glamorous, rich, and prosperous state.

But can we believe that the biblical narrators simply invented King David and his empire without having any ancient source to rely on? Or could they have had information about a historical king who did establish the empire between the Nile and Euphrates that they could have used as a model for David?

4

David's Empire

AS WE HAVE SEEN, there is no evidence to support the view that an empire stretching from the Nile to the Euphrates was founded in the early years of the tenth century BCE. Indeed, no such empire can be said to have been created between the time of Pharaoh Tuthmosis III in the fifteenth century BCE and the second half of the sixth century BCE, when Cyrus of Persia conquered both Mesopotamia and Egypt. Scholars have therefore had to explain—or rather explain away—the story of David's empire by saying that the biblical narrator simply invented it to aggrandize an important biblical figure.

DAVID'S TRUE IDENTITY

Although archaeologists have found no evidence to confirm the existence of David's empire in the tenth century BCE, they did find evidence of this same empire, only in a different time. It was established five centuries earlier than David's time by Pharaoh Tuthmosis III.

The Bible is notoriously suspect in its chronological sequences of events, doubtless as a result of the many centuries when its stories were passed down by word of mouth. Nevertheless, although the order in which they occurred is muddled in places, the account of David's wars as found in 2 Samuel is clearly dealing with the same events that are inscribed in the annals of Tuthmosis III recorded at Karnak. Attempting to conceal the early relationship between the tribes of Israel and pharaonic Egypt, the biblical scribes amalgamated the stories of two characters—one a warrior king who lived in the fifteenth century BCE, the other a tribal chief who lived five centuries later—to create the story of King David.

When we compare the Egyptian account of Tuthmosis III's wars in the Levant with the biblical account of David's wars, we can clearly see the similarities. First of all, 2 Samuel 8:3 tells us that David went to "recover his border at the river Euphrates," but the Bible gives us no account of David, or any Israelite leader, whose border extended to the Mesopotamian river. When Tuthmosis III went out to fight in the Levant, however, he did so precisely in order to recover his border at the Euphrates. Following the long, peaceful reign of Queen Hatshepsut of the Eighteenth Dynasty, Egypt realized that it had lost the empire that

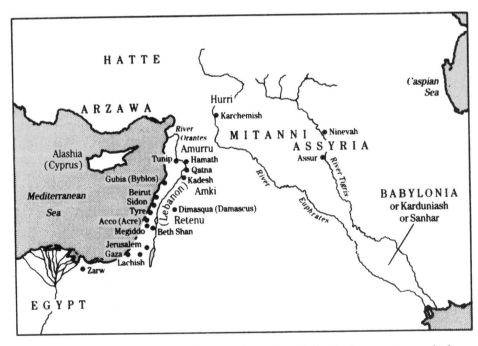

The empire of Tuthmosis III between the Nile and the Euphrates rivers, which would be used by Hebrew authors to describe the empire of King David

had been established earlier by Tuthmosis I. As soon as Tuthmosis III succeeded Hatshepsut, he went out to recover Egypt's lost borders in the Levant—up to the Euphrates.

The account of Tuthmosis III's wars at the Karnak temple, copied from the daily records of the scribe who accompanied the army on its campaigns, provides considerable light on the nature of David's alleged wars from Egyptian historical sources. They show how the events of Tuthmosis's reign were adapted by Hebrew scribes for the reign of David five centuries later. They reveal the significance of the battleground of Megiddo. They show how Jerusalem came to be known as the "royal" city of David and how David brought up the Ark (boat) of the Lord to Jerusalem (2 Samuel 6:1). They also uncover the origins of the name *Zion,* which has not been found in any historical source and makes its first appearance in the Bible with David's entry into Jerusalem: "David captured the fortress of Zion, the city of David" (2 Samuel 5:7).

TUTHMOSIS'S CAMPAIGN IN CANAAN

The Egyptian account begins with Tuthmosis III's departure at the head of his troops from the fortified border city of Zarw in northern Sinai during the last days of year 22 of his reign. Ten days later he arrived in Gaza, where he celebrated the start of his year 23 (1468 BCE) with festivals in honour of his "father," the god Amun-Ra, whose image he carried inside an ark at the head of the marching army. He stayed there for the night before pushing north toward central Canaan, where he paused in a town called Yehem to the south of a mountainous ridge he had to cross in order to reach Megiddo, where the Qadeshite (Syrian) enemy had gathered. At Yehem he was faced with a choice of three routes, but the shortest, called the Aruna road, was narrow and dangerous, so he summoned a council of war.

The king's officers were opposed to choosing the Aruna route. They said: "How can one go on this road which is so narrow? It is

reported that the enemy stand outside, and have become numerous. Will not horse have to go behind horse, and soldiers and people
likewise? Shall our own vanguard be fighting while the rear stands
here in Aruna [the starting point of the narrow road] and does not
fight?" However, in the light of fresh reports brought in by messengers, Tuthmosis III decided that he would make his way to Megiddo
by the unappealing—but to his enemies unexpected—narrow road, a
choice to which his officers replied: "Thy father Amun prosper thy
counsel. . . . The servant will follow his master."[1] Thus the scene was
set for the first battle of Megiddo.

In his assault upon Megiddo, Tuthmosis III marched at the head
of the narrow mountainous road from Aruna, with the image of
Amun leading the way. When he eventually emerged into the valley
southeast of the city, he could see that the enemy forces had been
divided (just as in the biblical account of the attack on Rabbah).
Having apparently expected him to take one of the two broader
roads available to him, one group had been stationed at Taanach to
the south and the other nearer to the walls of Megiddo. As a result
of his unexpected choice of route, Tuthmosis and his troops appeared
on the scene between them. On the advice of his officers, the king
encamped for two days while he waited for the rear echelon of his
army to arrive. Then, having divided his army into separate units,
he attacked: "His Majesty set forth in a chariot of fine gold, adorned
with his accoutrements of combat, like Horus, the Mighty of Arm, a
lord of action like Montu (Egyptian god of war), the Theban, while
his father Amun made strong his arm. The southern wing of His
Majesty's army was at a hill south of [the] Kina [brook], and the
northern was to the north-west of Megiddo, while His Majesty was
in their centre, Amun being the protection of his person."[2]

The Egyptian forces prevailed in the ensuing battle, and the kings
opposed to Tuthmosis fled to the sanctuary of fortified Megiddo,
where, as the gates of the city had been shut, they were hauled to safety

by citizens who let down "garments to hoist them up." The account of the battle complains that the enemy had "abandoned their horses and their chariots of gold and silver" and "if only His Majesty's army had not given up their hearts to capturing the possessions of the enemy, they would [have captured] Megiddo at this time."[3] Instead they had to lay siege to the city for seven months, the occupants having surrounded it with a protective ditch and fence: "They measured [this] city, which was corralled with a moat and enclosed with fresh timbers of all their pleasant trees." However, the king was not with them: "His Majesty himself was in a fortress east of this town."[4]

Although "Rabbahin," in eastern Jordan, is mentioned among the cities subdued by Tuthmosis, there is no indication that he personally conducted any military campaigns against Rabbah; it appears that this city, like many other Canaanite towns, sent tribute to the pharaoh without the need for war. But the details of Tuthmosis III's campaign against Megiddo strongly resemble those of David's battle against the fortified city of Rabbah (2 Samuel 11:1). According to the biblical account, the Ammonites of eastern Jordan and the Arameans (or Syrians), though allied, operated as separate units (2 Samuel 10:6). This echoes the description of the divided forces facing Tuthmosis III when he arrived unexpectedly by the Aruna road before his assault upon Megiddo. The escape of the Syrian king of Qadesh and his troops is reflected in the biblical account of the battle, where it says: "And when the children of Ammon saw that the Arameans were fled, they fled . . . and went into the city" (2 Samuel 10:14). There is also a parallel in the details of the subsequent siege: Tuthmosis III left the field of battle for "a fortress to the east," while we are told that "David tarried still at Jerusalem" (2 Samuel 11:1). Similarly, in the biblical narrative, the Ammonites wait near the gate of their city, while their Aramean allies wait further away in the open country. Then, as was the case at Megiddo, David's enemies fled and sought refuge in their city, which was then besieged. Unlike the Megiddo account found at Karnak,

2 Samuel 11:1 suggests that the subsequent siege of the city did not start until "after the year was expired," but, like the battle for Megiddo, it ended in triumph. Except for the time lapse between the battle and the siege, the biblical account of these events exactly matches the historical details of Tuthmosis's successful campaign against Megiddo.

This conclusion is reinforced by the fact that in the Bible, Solomon simply inherited David's empire without becoming involved in any military campaigns, and Megiddo is found among his possessions. In 1 Kings 9:15 we are told that one purpose of his raising a levy was "to build . . . the wall . . . of Megiddo," and it is also mentioned as one of his possessions in 1 Kings 4:12.

JERUSALEM IN TUTHMOSIS'S TIME

We know from the Bible that David "and his men marched to Jerusalem . . . [and] captured the fortress of Zion. . . . David then took up residence in the fortress and called it the City of David." No actual fighting between David and the Jebusites is reported, as his men entered the fortress through a water shaft (2 Samuel 5:6–7, 9).

On the other hand, we know that, after his allied enemies were defeated at Megiddo, Tuthmosis III went with his men to stay in a fortress *east* of Megiddo while his forces were laying siege on the city. As is the case with David when he went to Jerusalem, no fighting was needed for the king to enter this fortress. Although the name of the fortress where Tuthmosis stayed is not mentioned, this could only have been Jerusalem, the same place where David is said to have established his residence. Jerusalem, about seventy-nine miles southeast of Megiddo, was the only possible location for the pharaoh to have stayed for the seven months of the siege. Nevertheless, the name of Jerusalem was not included in the king's list for two reasons:

1. When Tuthmosis III went out to fight against the confederation of Canaanite and Syrian princes at Megiddo, Jerusalem was not part of

the rebellion. Tuthmosis faced no need to take control of the fortress by force. Instead he was able to make his way straight from Gaza to Megiddo and, without need for military action, to seek safe sanctuary in Jerusalem during the seven months in which Megiddo was under siege.

2. Although Jerusalem came under Egyptian control at that time, the name *Jerusalem* does not appear at all, neither in the western Asiatic city-list of Tuthmosis III nor in any lists of his immediate successors. This has not previously been explained. My own view is that Egyptians at the time recognized Jerusalem by another name—Qadesh (not to be confused with Syrian Qadesh on the river Orontes), which is a Semitic word meaning "holy." Among the historical records of Tuthmosis III found at Karnak, a list was found that includes more than a thousand names of Canaanite locations that fell under Egyptian control after his first Asiatic campaign. At the top of this list we find the name Qadesh in Canaan, which could not have been the same city as Qadesh in Syria. The modern Arabic name for Jerusalem is *al-Quds*. In Hebrew it is *ha-Qudesh,* which means "the holy place." This meaning is confirmed by the Bible, where Nehemiah 11:1 calls Jerusalem "the holy city" (*yerushalayim 'ir ha-qodesh* in Hebrew), which suggests that Jerusalem was known as "the holy city" in ancient times.

THE HOLY ARK

The account of bringing the ark to Jerusalem is found both in the biblical story of David and in the Egyptian records of Tuthmosis III. According to the Bible, shortly after David's arrival to Jerusalem, he "brought the ark of the LORD and set it in its place inside the tent that David had pitched for it" (2 Samuel 6:17). In the meantime, we know from his records that Tuthmosis brought the Ark of Amun-Ra with him from Egypt.

Although we have no recorded account, it is logical to assume that the king would have been accompanied to Jerusalem by the Ark of Amun-Ra, which had been carried at the head of his army as it advanced on Megiddo. We know that there were some rituals in Egyptian religion that only the king and high priest could perform before their deity. It is also logical to assume that the resting place for the ark would be Mount Moriah, the high ground to the north of the fortress, which had been revered as a holy place even before the time of Abraham. To this day, it is the setting for two of the holiest shrines of Islam, the Dome of the Rock and Al-Aqsa Mosque, as well as for the Jewish Wailing Wall.

We learn from 2 Samuel that David, who had remained in the fortress of Jerusalem, rejoined his forces to lead the final successful assault on the besieged city of Rabbah and then took "the crown from their king's head. . . . David took a great quantity of plunder from the city" (2 Samuel 12:30). David also took a large number of prisoners of war to work for him, and, before returning to Jerusalem, he subdued the rest of the Ammonite cities. Similarly, according to Egyptian texts, Tuthmosis III left his residence at the fortress and joined his forces to lead the final assault on Megiddo. He then moved north, to southern Lebanon, where he captured three cities by the river Litani before returning to Egypt.

THE FIRST ARMAGEDDON

We find a reflection of the memory of Tuthmosis's victory at Megiddo in Revelation 16:16. Here Armageddon (in Hebrew, *har Megiddon:* the mount of Megiddo) is designated as the site where, at the end of days, the kings of the world will fight the ultimate battle against the forces of God. This points to the belief that the Messiah, born of the House of David, will one day have to reenact the battle of his great ancestor who conquered Megiddo and that the final confrontation between good and evil will take place here.

Three cities—Megiddo, Hazor, and Gezer—are specifically mentioned in the Bible in connection with King Solomon's ambitious building activities (1 Kings 9:15).

David and his men marched north to Syria, on his way to "restore his monument [i.e., his boundary marker] at the Euphrates River." But before getting to the Euphrates, "David also defeated Hadadezer, king of Zobah." Although his army had footmen only, "David captured a thousand chariots, hundred charioteers and twenty thousand foot soldiers" (2 Samuel 8:3–4).

No trace of Zobah has been found in Syria or Canaan at the time of either David or Tuthmosis III. Yet this account fits in precisely with the sequence of events described in the wars of Tuthmosis. So although there has been some scholarly debate about the matter, the biblical city of Zobah is conventionally identified as Qadesh (not to be confused with the Qadesh that has been identified with Jerusalem).

Qadesh, the northern Syrian stronghold on the river Orontes during the Canaanite period, has been identified with the modern Tell Nebi Mend, south of Lake Homs. Together with Megiddo, Qadesh headed the coalition of Canaanite kings against Egypt, and, although confined with the other defeated kings within the walls of Megiddo, the king of Qadesh managed to escape and continued to lead rebellions against Egypt.

The book of 2 Samuel does not provide a date for David's alleged defeat of Hadadezer, but we know from the Karnak inscriptions that Tuthmosis captured Qadesh as part of his continuing campaign to restore his empire. The pharaoh then crossed the Euphrates in his year 33 (1458 BCE) and defeated the king of Mitanni: "My Majesty crossed to the farthest limits of Asia. I caused to be built boats of cedar on the hills of the God's Land [Phoenicia] in the neighborhood of the-mistress-of-Byblos [Ashtaroth]. They were placed on chariots [wheeled wagons], oxen dragging them, and they journeyed in front of My Majesty in order to cross that great river which flows between this country and Nahrin [Mitanni]. . . . Then My Majesty set up a stele on the mountain of Nahrin taken from the mountain on the west side of the Euphrates."5

Evidence of Tuthmosis's wars has been found by archaeologists excavating at the site of Qadesh. The evidence makes it clear that the final destruction of this Syrian stronghold took place five centuries before the biblical date for David's victories. It also showed that the fortified city of Qadesh no longer existed at the time of David in the early part of the tenth century BCE.

Archaeological evidence leaves no doubt that the only empire between the Euphrates in northern Syria and the Egyptian Sinai in the south was established by Tuthmosis III in the fifteenth century BCE. Until Cyrus of Persia in the sixth century BCE, this entire area did not fall under the control of any other empire. So why did the biblical narrators use the accounts of Tuthmosis III's wars in their David story?

5

The Chosen One

CLEARLY THE BIBLICAL NARRATORS did not invent the story of the great empire between the Euphrates and the Sinai. At the same time, the Egyptian account must have been part of the sources, written or oral, that they relied upon to write the David story; otherwise they would not have deliberately used it. On the other hand, why should the story of Tuthmosis III become part of the biblical sources about the history of the Israelites? The answer to this question will completely change what we know about the Hebrew family of Israel and its true ancestor.

Tuthmosis III, the son of a concubine, came to the throne of Egypt under strange circumstances around 1490 BCE. His name in Egyptian, Tehuti-mose, means "the son of Tehut," (Thoth, or Hermes in Greek). The Eighteenth Dynasty had been founded nearly a hundred years earlier after more than a century of rule over the eastern Delta of Egypt by the invading Hyksos, who were Semitic shepherds. At this point the princes of Thebes united in a successful attempt to drive them out of the country. This victory resulted in the crowning of Ahmosis I (ca. 1575–1550 BCE) as the first ruler of the Eighteenth Dynasty, which started what is known as the New Kingdom. In all, he spent fifteen years battling to ensure that no part of Egypt remained under foreign control, pursuing the remnants of the Hyksos into the Gaza region.

Ahmosis I was followed by his son, Amenhotep I (ca. 1550–1528 BCE), who pushed further into Canaan and Syria in continuing campaigns. He in turn was followed on the throne by Tuthmosis I (ca. 1528–1510 BCE), one of his generals, whom Amenhotep had arranged to marry the royal heiress, appointing him as his coregent. Despite his relatively short reign, Tuthmosis I was the founder of the Egyptian empire. He marched into western Asia at the head of his army and reached the Euphrates. There they succeeded in crossing the river into the territory of Mitanni (the ancient kingdom of northern Mesopotamia), where Tuthmosis erected a stele commemorating his victory. At this time, the Egyptians were satisfied simply with crushing their enemies and never tried to establish control over the vanquished territories.

The next ruler was the king's son, Tuthmosis II (ca. 1510–1490 BCE), born of a minor wife and not the Great Royal Wife, Queen Ahmose. As was the custom, in order to inherit the throne, he married his half sister, Hatshepsut, the daughter of his father and Queen Ahmose. In his turn, Tuthmosis II chose his son, Tuthmosis III (ca. 1490–1436 BCE), by a concubine named Isis, to be his successor, but Hatshepsut objected.

To ensure his son's right to the throne, Tuthmosis II took the precaution of having him adopted by the state god, Amun-Ra. The story of the god's choice of Tuthmosis III to be king is found in an inscription at Karnak, written long after he had come to the throne. It describes how the selection ceremony took place in the Temple of Amun at Thebes as the ark of the state god was carried in procession: "On recognizing me, lo, he [the god] halted. . . . [I threw myself on] the pavement, I prostrated myself in his presence. . . . Then they [the priests] [revealed] before the people the secrets in the hearts of the gods." At this point, the story describes how the young prince was whisked off to heaven to be appointed king by Ra, the king of the gods: "Ra himself established me. I was dignified with the diadems which were upon his head, his serpent diadem, rested upon [my forehead]. . . . I was sated with the counsels of the gods, like Horus . . . at the house of my father, Amun-Ra."[1]

Tuthmosis III, who had been given the throne name (the one given at his coronation, different from the one given at birth) Menkheper-Ra (established in the form of Ra), was still a young boy of about five when father died. His adoption by Amun-Ra as king would in the normal course of events have been confirmed by marriage to his half sister, Neferure, a daughter born to Queen Hatshepsut shortly before the death of Tuthmosis II. This marriage did not take place because of Hatshepsut's objection. Hatshepsut prevented the young king from ruling. Instead, she (his stepmother) appointed herself as his guardian, allowing him only to appear behind her in reliefs of the period.

So as early as Tuthmosis III's year 2 (1489 BCE), Hatshepsut even took the step of sharing the kingship, posing and being dressed as a man. For as long as she lived, she kept Tuthmosis III in the background, regarding her daughter, Neferure, as the real heiress. Hatshepsut was known as the "Lady of the Two Lands, Mistress of Upper and Lower Egypt" (a title found on inscriptions of Hatshepsut). Her plans were frustrated, however, when her daughter died in year 6 of the coregency, and from this point onward Tuthmosis III gained importance. He seems to have joined the Egyptian army as a young man, and there is evidence that he fought in the Gaza area toward the end of the coregency.

The chance for the young king to rule Egypt on his own came in the middle of year 22 (1469 BCE) of the coregency, when Hatshepsut died. It seems that the first task he undertook was to deface many of the monuments erected to his stepmother: her reliefs were hacked out, her inscriptions erased, her cartouches (the oval rings containing names and titles of Egyptian rulers) obliterated, her obelisks walled up. Now, even though he was the king's son, as he was not the son of the Egyptian queen but rather the son of a concubine, and he had not married the heiress to inherit the throne, technically he ruled only by virtue of having been chosen by the state god Amun-Ra. Nor was Tuthmosis III the legal descendant of the earlier Ahmosside Dynasty. From this time until the end of the Amarna rule in Egypt—the rule of Akhenaten, Semenkhkare, Tutankhamun, and Aye in the fourteenth century BCE—it was the dynasty chosen by the state god Amun-Ra and founded by Tuthmosis III that sat on the throne of Egypt.

The sarcophagus in the tomb of Tuthmosis III (no. 34 in the Valley of the Kings) was found to be empty when it was discovered. His mummy eventually came to light, together with thirty-two other royal mummies, hidden in a chamber three meters wide and nearly three hundred meters long at the bottom of a narrow shaft dug in the slopes of the necropolis of western Thebes. They had lain there for more than two thousand years, having been hidden by Egyptian priests who feared for their safety after many incidents of tomb robbing.

Yet modern robbers did find the new hiding place. The mummy of Tuthmosis III had been torn from its coffin and had suffered considerable damage as it was stripped of its jewels. The head, which had broken free from the body, showed that the king was almost completely bald at the time of his death, apart from a few short white hairs behind the left ear. All four limbs had also become detached from the torso, the feet had become detached from the legs, and both arms had been broken in two at the elbow: "Before re-burial some renovation of the wrapping was necessary and, as portions of the body became loose, the restorers, in order to give the mummy the necessary firmness, compressed it between four oar-shaped slips of wood. . . . Happily, the face, which had been plastered over with pith at the time of embalming, did not suffer at all from this rough treatment, and appeared intact when the protecting mask was removed."[2]

The author of these words, Gaston Maspero, director-general of the Cairo Museum at the time (1896), went on to say: "His statues, although not representing him as a type of manly beauty, yet give him

Tuthmosis III

refined, intelligent features, but a comparison with the mummy shows that the artists have idealised their model."[3]

In 1959, another view of the king's appearance was provided by the American scholar William C. Hayes: "Incontestably the greatest pharaoh ever to occupy the throne of Egypt, Tuthmosis III appears to have excelled not only as a warrior, a statesman and an administrator, but also as one of the most accomplished horsemen, archers and all-round athletes of his time. . . . [Yet] physically he cannot have been very pre-possessing. His mummy shows him to have been a stocky little man, under five feet four inches in height, and his portraits are almost unanimous in endowing him with the . . . most beaked of all the Tuthmossied noses."[4]

Tuthmosis III's physical appearance and lack of stature did not damage his domestic life. His chief wife and the mother of his successor, Amenhotep II (ca. 1436–1413 BCE), was his half sister, Meryt-Ra. Nothing much is known about her, but she was certainly not the heiress (which would have been only daughters of Pharaoh Tuthmosis II and Queen Hatshepsut). Additionally, in Egyptian traditions the throne is inherited by the heiress, the eldest surviving daughter of the older pharaoh. That is because Egyptians believed in the holy birth of the pharaoh as the son of Amun. Before going to bed with his bride, the pharaoh has to go through a ritual at the temple, where the priests ask for the spirit of Amun to dwell in the pharaoh's body. That is why they regard the newly born child as being physically the son of his father and spiritually the son of the god. However, if the pharaoh's bride was not the heiress, Amun would not come to dwell in the pharaoh's body. In addition, Tuthmosis III had at least three Asiatic wives and a large harem.

By the time that Tuthmosis III became sole ruler of Egypt following Hatshepsut's death, in his year 22, four decades had passed without a major Egyptian military campaign in western Asia. Now the situation changed completely. The king of Qadesh, a strong fortified city on the river Orontes in northern Syria, led a Syrio-Canaanite confederacy in a general rebellion against Egypt. In response, Tuthmosis III marched into western Asia to regain the territories between the Nile and Euphrates that had been conquered forty years earlier by his grandfather, Tuthmosis I. In the following twenty years, he led a total of seventeen campaigns in western Asia, at the end of which he had earned himself the reputation of being the mightiest of all the kings of the ancient world—and had reestablished his grandfather's empire.

The fact that the annals of Tuthmosis III found a place in the story of David means that the biblical editors wanted to hide the name of the true ancestor of the Israelite people. From a semantic point of view, the pharaoh's name poses no problem. It consists of two elements. In hieroglyphic writing, the first part, *tut* or *tw,* takes the form of an ibis, representing Thoth, the Egyptian god of wisdom and knowledge, and in transliteration into Hebrew becomes *Dwd,* which is the Hebrew name for David. The second element, *mos,* simply means "child" or "son." In fact, evidence suggests that it may have been the biblical editor who gave the tribal chief the name *Dwd.* Some scholars believe that this was not his original name; the *Encyclopaedia Judaica* states, "Elhanan was David's original name, which was later changed to David."[5] This idea is reinforced by the fact that Targum, the early translation of the Hebrew Bible into Aramaic, substitutes *Elhanan* for *David* in the account of how "Elhanan slew the brother of Goliath the Gittite, the staff of whose spear was like a weaver's beam" (2 Samuel 21:19).

6

Sarah and the Pharaoh

WHEN WE THINK OF THE ISRAELITES' CONNECTION with Egypt, we always talk about Joseph the patriarch, of the coat of many colors. It was he who brought Jacob—that is, Israel—and his Hebrew tribe from Canaan to Egypt. Nevertheless, the Bible itself gives us an account of an earlier Hebrew contact with Egypt's pharaonic family, by Abraham and his wife Sarah. Abraham the Hebrew, who made his first appearance in history in the fifteenth century BCE,* has been regarded by Jews, Christians, and Muslims alike as the founding father of the twelve tribes of Israel.

In this chapter, I am going to show that Abraham's patriarchy is by no means actual; rather, it is of symbolic importance to the Israelites and to their descendants and to Christians as well.

Abram and his wife Sarai (to give them their original names) began their journey into history, according to the biblical account, at Ur (modern Tell el-Muqayyar) in southern Mesopotamia, an important city two hundred miles southeast of present-day Baghdad. The party, led by Terah, Abraham's father, also included Lot, Terah's grandson and Abram's nephew. Genesis gives no explanation of why Terah and

---

*According to biblical chronology, Abraham lived during the nineteenth century BCE. The Hebrews did not appear in history before the fifteenth century BCE.

his family set out on the great trade route, which followed the valley of the Euphrates northwest through Babylon before sweeping west through Canaan to link with the ports of the eastern Mediterranean. Nor is there any indication of the date when this migratory journey began.

It is more than seven hundred miles from Ur to Canaan, which at that time occupied much the same area as modern Israel, the West Bank, and Gaza. The family made the journey in two stages, settling for an unspecified time at Haran in the middle of the valley of the Euphrates, where Terah died. We are then offered the first intimation of a special relationship between Abram's family and Yahweh. The Lord is said to have told Abram: "Go from your country . . . to the land I will show you. I will make you into a great nation" (Genesis 12:1–2).

In response to this promise, the family continued its journey south to the land of Canaan, a country where the sudden appearance of strangers was a common occurrence. Traders used its coastal plain for their commercial journeys south to, and north from, Arabia and Egypt. It also offered passage to armies during the recurrent imperial rivalries between Egypt in the south and the Mesopotamian kingdoms of Mitanni, Assyria, and Babylon in the north and east. In addition, in times of drought the country suffered recurrent mini-invasions by tribesmen from the neighboring Arabian desert.

For anyone trying to make a living from the soil, the hills of Canaan posed an intimidating challenge. The climate was hostile. In summer, the country was scorched by the sun and the hot, sand-laden sirocco wind. The late autumn rains, which made it possible to plow the baked soil, were followed by wet, and often bitterly cold, winters. Then as the sun grew in strength, the gentler rains of March and April provided a little fresh pasture for sheep, goats, and cattle before the onset of another dry season. Grain could be grown only on the coastal plain and in the valleys, and the staple agricultural products of the country—all that the inhospitably stony hills would support—were the olive and the vine. Times of famine were common, and it was at a time of famine that Abram and Sarai are said to have set out on their travels again from Haran, making their way south, a journey that was to forge the first links between this Hebrew Semitic tribe and the royal house of Egypt and ensured for Abram's family an enduring place in world history.

Compared with Canaan, Egypt was a rich and sophisticated country. Although the greater part of it was desert, the land on both sides of the Nile (watered by an intricate system of irrigation canals and dykes) and on the river's delta (flooded each year by the inundation that followed heavy rains and melting snows down in the Ethiopian highlands) were exceptionally fertile. The inundation, attributed to a teardrop from the goddess Isis, was a particularly important feature of Egyptian life. Religious festivals were held in her honor, and even today, June 17, the night when the Nile begins to flood, is known as "the night of the drop."

Major Egyptian crops included wheat (for bread), barley (for beer), vegetables, fruit (including grapes for wine), and flax (for linseed oil and linen thread). The soil was so rich that two crops could often be harvested in the same growing season. The Egyptians also kept pigs, goats, sheep, and ducks and could supplement their diet with fish from the Nile, wildfowl from the marshes, and game from the desert.

Although Abram and Sarai are said by the Bible to have set out for Egypt at a time of famine, it may have been some other motive—trade, perhaps—that caused them to make the journey. Certainly they did not stay in the eastern Delta of the Nile—which one might have expected had they simply been seeking food—but made their way to wherever the pharaoh of the time was holding court.

At this period, this could have been any one of three places—Memphis, Heliopolis, or Thebes. Memphis, twelve miles south of modern Cairo, was an important trade center, graced by the Great Temple of Ptah, patron of craftsmen and artisans. Heliopolis—known in the

Bible as On—was the original Egyptian holy city, situated a short distance to the north of modern Cairo and the chief center of worship of the sun god Ra. Both of these northern cities were used by the court to escape the worst of the blistering heat of an Egyptian summer. During the Eighteenth Dynasty (1575–1335 BCE), Heliopolis declined in importance as Thebes—modern Luxor, some 300 miles to the south, on the east bank of the Nile, opposite the Valley of the Kings, and the main center of worship of the state god Amun-Ra—developed into the main capital of the two lands of Egypt.

Wherever Abram and Sarai went, and for whatever purpose, we are told that Sarai was "a fair woman to look upon." As they approached Egypt, Abram, fearing that he might be killed if it were known that Sarai was his wife and the pharaoh took a fancy to her, said: "Say you are my sister, so that I will be treated well for your sake and my life will be spared because of you" (Genesis 12:13). This, according to Genesis,

James Tissot, Abram's Counsel to Sarai *(ca. 1896–1902)*

proved a wise precaution. Courtiers advised the pharaoh of the beau-tiful woman who appeared in their midst, and "she was taken into his palace. He treated Abram well for her sake, and Abram acquired sheep and cattle, male and female donkeys, male and female servants, and camels. But the LORD inflicted serious diseases on Pharaoh and his household because of Abram's wife Sarai. So Pharaoh summoned Abram. 'What have you done to me?' he said. 'Why didn't you tell me she was your wife? Why did you say, "She is my sister," so I took her to be my wife? Now then, here is your wife. Take her and go!' Then Pharaoh gave orders about Abram to his men, and they sent him on his way, with his wife and everything he had" (Genesis 12:15–20).

Abram and Sarai were sent back to Canaan with generous gifts. Pharaoh also provided Sarai with an Egyptian maid, Hagar, and, after they had returned safely to Canaan, Sarai gave birth to a son, Isaac. The essence of the biblical account of the journey to Egypt is that Sarai, the wife of Abram, also became the wife of the ruling pharaoh. This, in the custom of the time, would have involved not only paying the bride-price to Abram for the hand of his "sister," but sexual inter-course on the same day as the actual marriage ceremony. The question therefore arises: *who was the real father of Isaac, Abram or the pharaoh?*

The available evidence—the marriage; Abram posing as Sarai's brother; Sarai being seen by princes who commended her beauty to their king; her being taken into the royal palace; the king's marriage to her and his generous treatment of Abram; the gift to Sarai of the maid Hagar; the elaborate efforts of the biblical narrator to put as many years as possible between the couple's return to Canaan and Isaac's birth; tex-tual references in the Talmud and in the Qur'an; the history of Isaac's immediate descendants—points to the pharaoh, *not* Abram, as Isaac's father.

The efforts of the biblical narrator to disguise the truth about Isaac's parenthood have historical roots, I believe, that go beyond the fact that Isaac was the son of a second, "sinful" marriage. In the years that followed, the Israelites were to return to their ancestor's land in Egypt, where they remained for four generations until the Exodus, when, burdened by harsh treatment by their Egyptian taskmasters, they were led out of the country by Moses to the Promised Land back in Canaan. Many more centuries passed before an account of these events was put down in writing, by which time Egypt and its pharaoh had become symbols of hatred for the Israelites. The biblical narrator was therefore at pains to conceal any family connections between Israel and Egypt.

To return to the immediate story: The biblical narrator makes the point that Sarai was unable to have children. "So after Abram had been living in Canaan ten years, Sarai his wife took her Egyptian slave Hagar and gave her to her husband to be his wife" (Genesis 16:3). Shortly afterward, we learn that Hagar conceived, and an angel of the Lord appeared to her with the news that she would bear a son and name him Ishmael (Genesis 16:11).

Abram, we are told, was eighty-six when Ishmael was born. Another thirteen years are allowed to pass before the account of another divine visitation to Abram, which resulted in a change of name for him and Sarai: "No longer will you be called Abram; your name will be Abraham, for I have made you a father of many nations. I will make you very fruitful; I will make nations of you, and *kings* will come from you" (Genesis 17:5, 6; emphasis added). The Lord also said: "This is my covenant with you and your descendants after you . . . to keep. Every male among you shall be circumcised" (Genesis 17:10).

This command, which Abraham carries out, not only promises that the Hebrew tribe will become a great nation ruled by "kings" but also forges another link between the Hebrew tradition and Egypt. Until that time in history, Egypt was the only country among the Eastern nations to have adopted the custom of circumcision. (The practice had appeared early in Egyptian history, as can be seen from mummies.)

The kings to come are not to come from Abraham's other wives, however, but from Sarah: "Kings of peoples will come from her" (Genesis 17:16). *Sar* in Hebrew means "prince," and *sarah* is the feminine form, which can be translated as "queen."

On hearing that Sarah was to bear a child, Abraham "fell facedown; he laughed and said . . . 'Will a son be born to a man a hundred years old? Will Sarah bear a child at the age of ninety?'" God reassured him with the words, "Sarah will bear you a son, and you will call him Isaac. I will establish my covenant with him as an everlasting covenant for his descendants after him" (Genesis 17:17, 19). Earlier the Lord had promised, "To your descendants I give this land, from the river of Egypt to the great river, the Euphrates" (Genesis 15:18).

Even at that point the biblical narrator did not feel it prudent to introduce the birth of Isaac. He interpolated two more stories to dispel any possible doubt about the identity of Isaac's father by placing a longer gap between Sarah's departure from Egypt and the birth of her son. First, he described how Abraham sought to free his nephew Lot, who had been captured by some enemies. Then, we are told that on a visit to Gerar in southern Canaan, Abraham again took the precaution of claiming that Sarah was his sister. Despite her great age, Abimelech, the king of Gerar, fell in love with her and was about to marry her when the Lord warned him against it in a dream (Genesis 20:1–3). It is only after the passage of many years since the return from Egypt that we are finally allowed to learn of Isaac's birth, a year after the Lord's promise to Abraham.

The biblical chronology presented by the biblical narrator means that Ishmael must have been fourteen years older than Isaac. But this seems unreliable, because we learned that Sarah banished Hagar and Ishmael after she saw him "mocking" Isaac (Genesis 21:9). The narrative that follows indicates that Ishmael was not old enough to be able to walk, let alone mock anyone: "Abraham took some food and a skin of water and gave them to Hagar. He set them on her shoulder and then set her off with the boy. She went on her way and wandered in the Desert of Beersheba. When the water in the skin was gone, she put the boy under one of the bushes. Then she went off and sat down . . . she began to sob. God heard the boy crying, and the angel of God called to Hagar. . . . Lift the boy up and take him by the hand . . . and she saw a well of water. So she went and filled the skin with water and gave the boy a drink" (Genesis 21:9–19).

Although this story is not mentioned in the Qur'an, Islamic tradition agrees with it, representing Ishmael as a mere baby, carried by his mother and unable to move from the spot where she placed him, when a fountain of water appeared suddenly beneath his feet.

In the Bible, this tale is followed by an account of how Abraham took Isaac to the top of Mount Moriah, where he proposed to sacrifice him as a burnt offering—a curious decision if Isaac had been his own son, given the Lord's promise to establish his covenant with Abraham's descendants. At the end, the Lord's angel warns him: "Do not lay your hand on the boy," and Abraham sacrifices a sheep instead (Genesis 22:9–12).

Indications that Isaac was a prince of Egypt do not depend solely on this analysis of Genesis. Nonbiblical sources point out that Abraham— who had seven other sons (Ishmael by Hagar and six by another wife, Keturah)—was regarded as the *adoptive* father of Isaac. The Talmud preserves a tradition that nobody knew Abraham believed that Isaac was his son: "On the day that Abraham weaned his son Isaac, he made a great banquet, and all the people of the world derided him, saying: 'Have you seen that old man and woman who brought a foundling from the street, and now claim him as their son . . . ?'"[1]

A verse in the Qur'an (21:72) says of Abraham: "We bestowed on him Isaac and, as an additional gift, [a grandson], Jacob."

The verse indicates that Isaac and Jacob, the grandson who had not been born when Abraham died, were not his originally. Another verse of the Qur'an (19:58), having mentioned three of the prophets—Moses, Aaron, and Ishmael—speaks of them as being "the posterity of Abraham and Israel"—that is, Jacob.

The only possible explanation of this verse is that some of these prophets—Moses, Aaron, and Ishmael—were descendants of Jacob, but *not* of Abraham. To elaborate on this point, we have two named ancestors (Abraham and Jacob) and three named descendants (Moses, Aaron, and Ishmael). It is obvious that had Jacob been a descendant of Abraham, he would have been named in the list of descendants rather than as an ancestor together with Abraham.

Who, then, was the Egyptian pharaoh who married Sarah and fathered Isaac?

All evidence points to Tuthmosis III. This is the same king who established David's supposed empire in the fifteenth century BCE. It was during Tuthmosis's reign that the Hebrews started to infiltrate the land of Canaan and visit Egypt. According to biblical scholar B. D. Eerdmans, the word *Hebrews* is identical with the word *Apriw* "found in Egyptian inscriptions, at least as early as the reign of Tuthmosis III."[2]

The real father of Isaac, and his Israelite descendants, was a pharaoh. So we can see why, from Isaac's birth up to the present day, a child cannot be regarded as a Jew, no matter who the father may have been, unless the mother is Jewish. We can also see why Abraham tried to sacrifice Isaac on the altar, and why the Lord promised to establish kings from among his descendants. Being the descendants of the great Egyptian pharaoh, they were to inherit his empire between the border of Egypt and the Euphrates.

7

Jerusalem, City of David

JERUSALEM OFFERS THE CLEAREST EVIDENCE about King David's identity. It is situated in the Judean hills, thirty-five miles east of the Mediterranean, at an elevation of 2,440 feet. Its first settlement dates back to the Stone Age, when families dwelt in caves in the vicinity, and there is evidence of continuity of settlement since the Early Bronze Age in the third millennium BCE.

Jerusalem began as an obscure fortress on the southeast hill, which could be seen from the neighboring heights. Today it consists of an ancient walled Old City and a New City. The present walls of the Old City, to which seven gates provide access, were last restored and rebuilt by the Ottoman sultan Suleiman the Magnificent in the first half of the sixteenth century CE. The New City, which extends outside the walls, was largely built after 1860.

The Bible describes the taking of Jerusalem as a military operation carried out by David: "The king and his men marched to Jerusalem to attack the Jebusites who lived there. . . . David then took up residence in the fortress and called it the City of David. He built up the area around it, from the supporting terraces inward" (2 Samuel 5:6, 9).

However, the evidence makes it clear that this operation was actually a peaceful one, carried out by Tuthmosis III, five centuries earlier.

The link between Tuthmosis III and Jerusalem derives from

the time when he based himself there while his army was besieging Megiddo. His annals, as we saw earlier, said that he stayed at a fortress east of Megiddo. Although the name of the fortress is not mentioned in the Egyptian text, indications are that Jerusalem, which lies to the southeast of Megiddo, is the location meant here. Leaving the besieged city and traveling east, the only route was the Way of the Sea, which is joined near the river Jordan by the road leading south to Jerusalem. It seems that Egyptian sources provide an incomplete account of the fortress where the king stayed because the scribe concerned remained with the army, recording details of the military campaign at Megiddo rather than accompanying the king.

THE ARK OF AMUN

Shortly after David's arrival, we have a description of how "they brought the ark of the LORD and set it in its place inside the tent that David had pitched for it, and David sacrificed burnt offerings . . . before the Lord" (2 Samuel 6:17). It is said that bringing the ark to Jerusalem made the city the holy center for the Israelite tribes. However, given what we have already seen, we are dealing not only with two Davids but with two arks—the Ark of the Covenant, in which Moses placed the Ten Commandments, and the ark in which Tuthmosis III carried his god, Amun-Ra, into battle before him at Megiddo, as described in the annals at Karnak: "Year 23, first month of the third season, day 19—awakening in [life] in the tent of life, prosperity and health, at the town of Aruna. Proceeding northward by my majesty, carrying my father Amun-Ra, Lord of the Thrones of the Two Lands [that he might open the ways] before me."[1]

It is clear that the idea of a holy ark was introduced to the Israelites by Moses from Egyptian worship practices. In festivals and on other occasions, the Egyptian deity used to be carried by the priests in an ark. When the king went to live in the fortress of Jerusalem at the start of the protracted siege of Megiddo, the only possible location for the god Amun-Ra in his ark was where the king was in residence. In fact, we know that there were some daily rituals in Egyptian worship that only the king and high priest could perform before the deity.

Here again we have no account either in the Bible or in Egyptian records of the king using any force to obtain the holy ground of Jerusalem for the ark. The Bible gives details of a peaceful transaction whereby Araunah, the Jebusite king of Jerusalem, sold David his threshing floor for fifty shekels of silver so that he could build an altar. In the course of these negotiations Araunah said to David: "Behold, here are oxen for the burnt offering, and here are threshing sledges and ox yokes for wood. O king, Araunah gives all this to the king" (2 Samuel 24:22–23). The choice of a threshing floor may seem a curious one for the site of an altar, but such elevated and exposed pieces of ground at the approaches to cities were often the site of cultic observances.

The sanctity of Jerusalem is implied in Genesis, which describes how Abraham received a blessing on this same piece of ground: "And Melchizedek king of Salem [Jerusalem] brought out bread and wine. He was priest of God Most High, and he blessed Abram, and said, Blessed be Abram by God Most High, Creator of heaven and earth. And blessed be God Most High, who delivered your enemies into your hand" (Genesis 14:18–20). Therefore, at least from the time of Abraham, this high ground to the north of Jerusalem had been regarded as holy, not just for the inhabitants of the city but for other peoples in Canaan as well.

But the threshing floor was not bought by the tribal David to build an altar for the Lord, but by Tuthmosis III as the site for a shrine to his state god, Amun-Ra. This is made clear in Psalms where David, like Egyptian kings, is called the Son of God: "I have installed my King on Zion, my holy hill. I will proclaim the decree of the LORD: He said to me, 'You are my son; today I have become your father.' Ask of me, and

I will make the nations your inheritance, the ends of the earth your possession" (Psalms 2:6–8).

The new name of Zion makes its first appearance in the Bible when we learn of King David's entry into Jerusalem: "David captured the fortress of Zion, the City of David" (2 Samuel 5:7). It assumes more importance from this time onward.

The name *Zion* is not always used to indicate the same location. In some cases, as in 2 Samuel 5:7, it seems to signify the fortress of Jerusalem. Yet at the same time it is suggested that the fortress was named after the king: "David then took up residence in the fortress and called it the City of David" (2 Samuel 5:9). In other cases, *Zion* refers only to the sacred area that was used to build the Temple: "Then you will know that I, the LORD your God, dwell in Zion, my holy hill. Jerusalem will be holy; never again will foreigners invade her" (Joel 3:17). Here, while *Zion* refers clearly to the holy area of the Temple Mount, Jerusalem is clearly separate. There are also these verses: "May the LORD answer you when you are in distress; may the name of the God of Jacob protect you. May he send you help from the sanctuary and grant you support from Zion" (Psalm 20:1–2). It is clear in this case that by *Zion* only the sanctuary is meant.

Further complications arise from the fact that Mount Zion was later believed not to have been in the area of the Temple, high to the north of ancient Jerusalem, but on the western mount. Here, in the first century CE, a small church was built on the southern end of the hill, which became identified as the Coenaculum (the room of the Last Supper). This was followed many centuries later—in 1936—by a Christian monastery known today as the Church of Mary. Nevertheless, modern archaeology has confirmed that this western mount did not form part of ancient Jerusalem and was not occupied at the time of the tribal chief David.

All the indications are, in fact, that Zion, the ancient holy ground of Jerusalem, was the artificially flattened ground on Mount Moriah where Solomon built his Temple and which today includes two of the holiest shrines of Islam—the Dome of the Rock and Al-Aqsa Mosque. The Temple area is surrounded by the colossal Herodian enclosure wall, preserved in the east, south, and west; a larger section of the western wall (the Wailing Wall), which survives today, is the most venerated site in the Jewish tradition. In ancient times, even before David entered the fortress, this area was regarded as holy ground not only by the Jebusites but by Abraham. In fact, Mount Moriah is identified as the area where the Temple was first built: "Then Solomon began to build the temple of the Lord at Jerusalem on Mount Moriah, where the Lord appeared to his father David" (2 Chronicles 3:1). It is the same location where, in the account of Abraham's intention to slay Isaac, we have this obscure reference: "And Abraham called the name of that place The Lord Will Provide. And to this day it is said 'On the mountain of the Lord it will be provided'" (Genesis 22:14). As we have seen, Abraham also received the blessing from the king Melchizedek on the same holy ground.

However, it was when King David brought his ark and placed it here that this ancient holy ground was transformed into a holy center believed to be the abode of the Lord: "For the Lord has chosen Zion, he has desired it for his dwelling: 'This is my resting place for ever and ever: here I will sit enthroned, for I have desired it'" (Psalm 132:13–14). Once Tuthmosis III had taken the image of Amun-Ra in his ark to Jerusalem, the logical resting place for it, it was on the holy high ground of Mount Moriah where, one would expect, Tuthmosis III would have worshipped during his seven-month stay.

DAVID'S HOLY ARK

Whose ark was brought to Jerusalem?

Shortly after David's arrival in Jerusalem, the Bible speaks about bringing a holy ark to the city: "They brought the ark of the Lord and set it in its place inside the tent that David had pitched for it, and David sacrificed burnt offerings . . . before the LORD" (2 Samuel 6:17). However, if these events actually took place in the fifteenth century BCE, this object could not have been the Ark of the Covenant but would have been the Ark of Amun, brought by Tuthmosis III.

I believe this "Ark of the Lord" is not the same one as the Ark of the Covenant, although it could be similar. The Bible describes the Ark of the Covenant as a gold-covered wooden chest containing the two stone tablets of the Ten Commandments. When the Israelites came out of Egypt into Sinai, the Lord said to Moses to ask the Israelites to "make a chest of acacia wood. . . . Overlay it with pure gold, both inside and out. . . . Then . . . put in the ark the Testimony [the tablets of the Ten Commandments], which I will give you" (Exodus 25:10–11, 16).

While Moses was on Mount Sinai receiving the Ten Commandments, the Israelites persuaded his elder brother, Aaron, to make them an idol in the shape of a calf. The following morning they celebrated with a big feast, worshipping the idol. When Moses came down and saw this, "his anger burned and he threw the tablets out of his hands, breaking them to pieces at the foot of the mountain" (Exodus 32:19).

Later, when the Tabernacle, the tent of meeting, was completed, "the LORD said to Moses: 'Chisel out two stone tablets like the first ones, and I will write on them the words that were on the first tablets, which you broke. Be ready in the morning, and then come up on Mount Sinai. Present yourself to me there on the top of the mountain'" (Exodus 34:1–3).

After the death of Moses, the Ark of the Covenant is said to have been taken to the Promised Land by Joshua, who succeeded Moses as the leader of the Israelites. There, for the next three hundred years, the ark is said to have been moved from one location to the other in Canaan, including Gilgal near Jericho (Joshua 4:19), where it is believed to have remained for about seven years before it was moved to Shiloh, midway between Dan in the north and Beer-Sheba in the south (Joshua 18:1). After about three hundred and fifty years, during which time nothing was reported about the fate of the ark, the Philistines took the ark (1 Samuel 4:11). Later, after King Saul's death, when David became the king over all Israel, he decided to bring the ark of God from Judah to Jerusalem (2 Samuel 6:2).

I believe the Ark of the Covenant never went to the Promised Land, as the book of Joshua seems to be a fiction written by the priests and disagrees completely with the account of the book of Judges. Exposed wood does not last. Unless it is regularly treated it rots and decays. Many such wooden arks made in ancient Egypt disappeared with time, except those that were kept inside secure tombs. It is significant that here the Bible does not speak of the "Ark of Covenant" but of the "Ark of God." As I have mentioned before, it was Tuthmosis III, historical David, who brought the ark of his god, Amun, into Jerusalem.

It seems that, while attributing the military victories of Tuthmosis to David, the biblical scribe wanted also to include the account of the pharaoh's ark in David's story. However, in the fifteenth century BCE, more than a hundred years before the time of Moses and the Exodus, the Ark of the Covenant had not yet been made. The only ark that we know from historical sources to have reached Jerusalem at that time was the Ark of Amun, which was brought to the city by Tuthmosis III. When Tuthmosis left Jerusalem, he obviously must have taken the Ark of Amun with him back to Egypt.

Although Solomon is said to have placed the Ark of the Covenant inside the Temple he built in Jerusalem, after Solomon's death and the collapse of his empire, there is no more mention of the ark for more than three hundred years. An account of King Josiah (641–609 BCE) indicates that the ark was not in the Temple at that time, because he asks the Levites to "put the sacred ark inside the house that Solomon . . . built" (2 Chronicles 35:3).

Moreover, it is clear that the very idea of a holy ark was introduced to the Israelites by Moses from Egyptian practices of worship. In his festivals and on other occasions, Amun used to be carried by the priests in an ark. This custom is shown in the Anubis shrine found in Tutankhamun's tomb, with the jackal-like statue of Anubis, guardian of the dead, sitting on the top of a large box. Although the dimensions do not match, the Anubis shrine corresponds to the description of the Ark of the Covenant. It is covered with pure gold and has poles of acacia wood inserted into four rings on its sides. The similarities among these objects may be evidence that the biblical scribes used Egyptian sources to describe the Ark of the Covenant, or that the Israelites did not originate the idea of the ark but rather were introduced to the practice by Egyptians, through Moses. The ark brought by David into Jerusalem was not the Ark of the Covenant made by Moses, but the ark of the god Amun brought by Tuthmosis III.

HOLY ZION

After Tuthmosis III left Jerusalem at the end of his seven-month stay, the holy ground where he had worshipped became Egyptianized. This can be seen from the name it acquired: Zion. The name *Zion,* as we have seen, makes its first appearance in the Bible as soon as we learn of David's entry into Jerusalem and has not been found in any other historical source.

Although the word *Zion* occurs over 150 times in the Bible, the reason for using this name as a synonym for *Jerusalem* has not been explained. Its origins actually point to a link with Egypt. *Zion* (*tsiyyon*) is not originally a Hebrew word. It consists of two elements, one Semitic, the other Egyptian. The Semitic first element, *tsi,* means a "land of drought," a "barren place." But the meaning of the second Egyptian element has hitherto escaped recognition.

On is the biblical name of the Egyptian holy city of Heliopolis, a short distance to the north of modern Cairo. It is mentioned in the life of Joseph the patriarch: the pharaoh, having appointed Joseph to a high position, gave him an Egyptian wife, "the daughter of Potiphera, priest of On" (Genesis 41:45). After the decline of Heliopolis, when Thebes in Upper Egypt became the new capital city of the empire as well as the holy city of the state god, Amun-Ra, it became the custom to refer to Thebes as "the southern On" and Heliopolis as "the northern On," with *on* being used in the sense of "holy city." Thus the word *Si-on* or *Zi-on* means "holy city of the desert," its second syllable revealing its Egyptian origin.

Mount Moriah, until then holy only to the inhabitants of Jerusalem, became holy for all the Asiatic kingdoms of the Egyptian empire after Tuthmosis III made it his religious base during the siege of Megiddo and worshipped his god, Amun-Ra, there. After his seven-month stay, Tuthmosis III returned to Megiddo for his successful assault on the city, then made his way back home to Thebes. We have no means of knowing whether he visited Jerusalem again during one of his many campaigns in western Asia. Nevertheless, his descendants, the children of Sarah, never entirely forgot their great ancestor. After leaving Egypt and eventually settling in the Promised Land of Canaan, they made his holy ground the most venerated part of their new home.

8

David and Bathsheba

THE SIMILARITIES BETWEEN THE STORIES of Abraham and David are reflected in the fact that both of them married a woman who was married to another man. While, as we saw before, Pharaoh Tuthmosis III married Sarah, Abraham's wife, David is reported to have had sexual relation with Bathsheba, the wife of another man, and eventually married her.

The story of David in 2 Samuel tells us that while he was staying in Jerusalem during the siege of Rabbah, he saw Bathsheba bathing and made inquiries about her identity. On learning that she was the wife of Uriah the Hittite, who was serving with the king's forces at the siege, David sent messengers to bring her to his house where "he slept with her" (2 Samuel 11:4). As a result of this liaison, Bathsheba became pregnant. In the hope of disguising his guilt, David had Uriah, her husband, brought to Jerusalem, but the warrior refused to sleep in the comfort of his own house while the king's army was suffering the hardships of living in tents before the besieged city. David therefore sent him back to the battle with orders that he should be placed in a dangerous position so that he would be killed in the fighting.

After the mourning period for Uriah, David married his beloved Bathsheba, who bore him a son. "But the thing that David had done displeased the LORD" (2 Samuel 11:27).

This last verse and the first twenty-five verses of the chapter that follows are clearly a later insertion, because they have the prophet Nathan being sent by the Lord to reprove David for his sin. They go on to describe the illness and death of the unnamed child born to Bathsheba and the birth of another son to be called Solomon. Then 2 Samuel 12:26 resumes the account of the siege of Rabbah, culminating with its fall.

Abraham and Uriah, the two husbands in these stories, have similar backgrounds. Both are foreigners: Abraham is a Canaanite in Egypt, Uriah a Hittite in Jerusalem. In each case their wives are made pregnant by a king and give birth to a son, who has to die because he is the fruit of sin. However, the Genesis account is told without comment, and it is the pharaoh himself who sends Sarah away on discovering that she is already married to another man. In contrast, in 2 Samuel we see later concepts of morality enforcing judgments on the characters. The relationship between David and Bathsheba is regarded as adultery, with Uriah sent to his death to remove him from the scene. Whereas in Genesis, Isaac's life is spared and a sheep is sacrificed in his stead, in 2 Samuel the child has to die. The king is threatened with future troubles as a punishment; it is only the woman who escapes punishment. Nonetheless, in both cases, the line of descendants from the sinful relationship is promised to rule an empire between Egypt and the Euphrates.

Hermann Gunkel, the great German biblical scholar, dismissed the story of Uriah and his wife as having no historical basis. I believe its basis lies in the Pharaoh-Sarah-Abraham narrative in Genesis. If we examine the name *Uriah,* we find that it is composed of two elements—*ur,* a Hurrian (northern Mesopotamian) word meaning "city" or "light," and *yah,* which is the short form of the name of the Israelite god, Yahweh. The meaning of the name could therefore be "Yahweh's light." Yet he is described as being a Hittite. How can we expect one of the Hittites, traditional enemies of the Hebrews, to be a hero in David's army? Moreover, we are not given an explanation of the sudden appearance of this foreigner and his wife in the City of David.

In fact, the names *Uriah* and *Bathsheba* are alterations of *Abraham* and *Sarah*. To look at the matter from another point of view, fictional names usually give some indication of the original character who inspired them. *Ur,* the first part of Uriah's name, relates him to the city of Ur, the birthplace of Abraham. The Bible describes how "Terah took his son Abram, . . . and his daughter-in-law Sarai, . . . and together they set out from Ur of the Chaldeans to go to Canaan" (Genesis 11:31). Here *Ur of the Chaldeans* could mean either "a city of the Chaldees" or, if *Ur* was used as a proper noun, "Ur of the Chaldeans." In any case, later on *Ur* became a proper noun indicating the birthplace of Abraham. Thus the name *Uriah* relates this invented character both to Abraham's God and to his city of origin.

We have a similar situation with the name *Bathsheba*. Here also we have two elements—*bath,* meaning "girl" or "daughter," and *Sheba,* referring to an area in the south of Canaan that takes its name from the local well, Beersheba. The name *Bathsheba* can therefore be interpreted to mean "girl of Sheba," referring to Sarah, who, with her husband, settled in Beersheba after their return from Egypt (Genesis 21:31).

Although the tradition of David-Bathsheba-Uriah was a legendary composition based on the memory of Pharaoh-Sarah-Abraham, there is a possibility that Abraham might have met the pharaoh again in Jerusalem. The story describes two incidents that would make this possible.

The first incident could have taken place when Abraham went to Jerusalem (Salem) and was blessed by the priest and king Melchizedek (Genesis 14:19). This blessing must have taken place on the holy ground of Mount Moriah, later the site of the Temple. The second incident refers to the occasion when Abraham, being tested by God, was instructed to sacrifice Isaac on Mount Moriah (Genesis 22:2).

The purpose of Abraham's visit to Jerusalem, which does not fit in with the general development of the story, is not clear, but John Gray is one scholar who has suggested that it was connected with David: "The significance of the incident (the threatened sacrifice of Isaac), which is probably out of context, is uncertain, and it probably served a particular purpose of the compiler of the time of David and Solomon. This has been thought to be the authentication of David's adoption of the local cult of El Elyon (God Most High)."[1] A possible sequence of the events that lie behind Abraham's visit to Jerusalem would be as follows:

After leaving Egypt, Abraham and Sarah settled in Canaan, where Isaac was born. Later, in the course of his first Asiatic campaign, Tuthmosis III set up residence in the fortress of Jerusalem, waiting for Megiddo to surrender. On learning this, Abraham took Isaac, the pharaoh's son, to Jerusalem to present him to his father, threatening to kill the child. The king, while warning Isaac not to go down to Egypt, persuaded Abraham to abandon this course of action by a promise of some land in Canaan if he would agree to bring up Isaac as his own son. This sequence of events would explain why Bathsheba's first baby was unnamed in the Uriah-David-Bathsheba version of the story. This does not ring true, because it was normal at the time for Hebrew children to be named as soon as they were delivered. The narrator, eager to conceal the true facts about the parenthood of Isaac, and aware that he had not been put to death, invented the story of the child of sin who died, and left him unnamed.

9

Goliath the Giant

IN ORDER TO MAKE IT ACCEPTABLE for the young tribal shepherd to become a great military warrior, the biblical narrator felt the need to present the young lad as having superhuman power granted by God. Although, as we have seen, the biblical authors used the account of Tuthmosis III as a basis for the story of David, the tale of the slaying of Goliath does not belong to the Egyptian king.

At the beginning, we are told that David, the youngest son of Jesse from Bethlehem, is introduced to Saul as a shepherd and harpist, and Saul appoints him as his armor bearer (1 Samuel 16:25). Yet in the very next chapter we find this same David transformed into a mighty warrior at the head of Saul's army, encamped on a mountain on one side of the valley Elah, midway between Bethlehem and the Philistine Mediterranean coast. From the Philistine camp on an opposite mountain emerged Goliath with an offer to settle the whole conflict by man-to-man combat: "A champion named Goliath, who was from [the Philistine city of] Gath, came out of the Philistine camp. He was over nine feet tall. He had a bronze helmet on his head and wore a coat of scale armor of bronze weighing five thousand shekels; on his legs he wore bronze greaves, and a bronze javelin was slung on his back. His spear shaft was like a weaver's rod, and its iron point weighed six hundred shekels. His shield bearer went ahead of him"

(1 Samuel 17:4–7). This mighty fighter asked the Israelites to choose a champion and promised, "If he is able to fight and kill me, we will become your subjects" (1 Samuel 17:9).

At this point the story of the confrontation between the Philistines and the Israelites is interrupted by a passage, 1 Samuel 17:12–29, that is not found in the Septuagint, the ancient Greek version of the Bible dating from the third century BCE. Here we start from the beginning, before David meets King Saul. David, at the age of fifteen, is the youngest of the eight sons of Jesse of Bethlehem. Jesse asks him to take food to his three elder brothers, who have joined Saul's forces against the Philistines, in the battlefield. David's arrival in the camp coincides with Goliath's reappearance to repeat his challenge to the Israelites. When the young lad hears that Saul is willing to shower riches on anyone who kills the Philistine, and to give him his daughter in marriage, David volunteers to challenge Goliath. However, David's eldest brother is distressed by this news, and Saul tries to dissuade him from taking up the challenge. At this point the story resumes to follow the same account as the Greek text.

David insists on fighting Goliath and says to Saul: "Your servant has been keeping his father's sheep. When a lion or a bear came and carried off a sheep from the flock, I went after it, struck it and recued the sheep from its mouth. When it turned on me, I seized it by its hair, struck it and killed it. Your servant has killed both lion and bear; this uncircumcised Philistine will be like one of them, because he has defied the armies of the living God. The Lord who rescued me from the paw of the lion and the paw of the bear will rescue me from the hands of this Philistine" (1 Samuel 17:34–37). This oration convinces Saul, who says to David: "Go, and the Lord be with you."

Being so sure of his power, David refuses to wear armor or carry a sword into the conflict. Instead he goes out to face Goliath with his staff, a sling, and five smooth stones. The affronted giant demands: "Am I a dog, that you come to me with sticks? . . . Come here, . . . and

I'll give your flesh to the birds of the air and the animals of the field"
(1 Samuel 17:43–44).

With confidence, David replies: "You come against me with
sword and spear and javelin, but I come against you in the name
of the Lord. . . . This day the Lord will deliver you into my hands"
(1 Samuel 17:45–47).

David *by Michelangelo (1501–1504);*
photograph by Jörg Bittner Unna

In the familiar story that follows, David fells Goliath with a stone from his sling, takes the Philistine's sword, and cuts off his head. On seeing this, the Philistine forces flee, pursued by the Israelites, who subsequently return to plunder the Philistine camp. We are then told, "David took the Philistine's head and brought it to Jerusalem, and he put the Philistine's weapons in his own tent" (1 Samuel 17:54). But the story does not explain how David is able to take Goliath's head to Jerusalem before he has captured the city.

In the Greek text, the story of David's slaying of Goliath ends here. However, the Masoretic text—a later version of the Hebrew text, dating from the late first millennium CE, which is the basis of our English version of the Old Testament—contains four more verses. In this account, David does not ask Saul's permission to fight the Philistine; in fact, David does not even meet Saul until he has slain Goliath: "As Saul watched David going out to meet the Philistine, he said to Abner, commander of the [Israelite] army, '. . . whose son is that young man?' Abner replied, 'As surely as you live, I don't know.' The king said, 'Find out whose son this young man is.' As soon as David returned from killing the Philistine, Abner . . . brought him before Saul, with David still holding the Philistine's head. 'Whose son are you, young man?' Saul asked him. David said, 'I am the son of your servant Jesse of Bethlehem'" (1 Samuel 17:55–58). This indicates that there was more than one account available for the biblical editor to choose from.

Furthermore, there are a number of differences in this story even in various versions of 1 Samuel. Portions of this book were among the biblical manuscripts found in the caves of Qumran near the northwestern end of the Dead Sea after the Second World War. The text of the Qumran version, which cannot be later than the first century CE, has proved to correspond more closely to the Septuagint, which seems to have relied on a more accurate Hebrew tradition relating the story of Goliath. It seems that the Goliath story in the Septuagint came from an earlier Hebrew source, when it was still treated as a separate account that was not yet completely woven into the general narrative of the lives of Saul and David.

In fact, the Goliath tale does not originally belong to the stories of either the biblical David or Tuthmosis III. It was borrowed from an ancient Egyptian literary work known as *The Autobiography of Sinuhe*. In order to make it possible for the young shepherd to become a great warrior king, the biblical editor felt the need to build up his qualities as a brave and courageous fighter. He therefore incorporated the Sinuhe legend, which had nothing in it relating to David or his time.

THE AUTOBIOGRAPHY OF SINUHE

Sinuhe was a courtier in the service of Nefru, daughter of Amenemhat I, the founder of the Twelfth Dynasty in the twentieth century BCE. The form in which his autobiography is cast—the story of his sudden flight from Egypt, his wanderings, his battle with a mighty man like Goliath, and his eventual return to be buried in the land of his birth—makes it clear that it was written originally to be placed in his tomb. Many copies of the story, which is recognized as being based on historical facts, were found subsequently, dating from the twentieth century BCE, when the events actually occurred, until as late as the eleventh century BCE. It was a popular tale in ancient Egypt, taught as a literary examplar to students, and there can be no doubt that all educated persons in Egypt, no matter what their ethnic background, would have been familiar with its contents.

The story begins around 1960 BCE, year 30 and the last of Amenemhat I's reign. Sinuhe is at the time absent from the capital with the Egyptian army, led by the king's eldest son, his heir and coregent, Sesostris. While the army is making its way back from campaigns against Libyan tribes in the western Delta, a messenger arrives during the night with news that causes Sesostris to leave his troops immediately and set out for the palace. Messages have also been sent to younger sons of the king serving with the army, and Sinuhe overhears one of them being read aloud. It says there has been a palace conspiracy: an unsuccessful attempt has been made on the life of Amenemhat I while he slept.

On hearing this, Sinuhe becomes so afraid that he decides to run away. He does not say why he is afraid. In fact, at one point in his story he is at some pain to make it clear that there was no reason for him to run away at all, although, as one of the palace courtiers, he could well have been indirectly involved, or at least there could have been grounds for suspecting his involvement.

Later, in reporting a conversation with Nenshi, the son of Amu and the ruler of Upper Retenu (northern Canaan), he says that Nenshi asked: "'Why have you come here? Has anything happened at the residence?' and he replied, 'The King of Upper and Lower Egypt, Sehetepibre [Amenemhat I], has departed to the horizon [died] and no one knows what happened because of it. . . . When I returned from an expedition in the land of the Libyans, someone announced it to me. My mind reeled. My heart was not in my body, and it brought me to the path of flight. Yet no one had spoken about me; no one spat in my face. No reviling word was heard, nor was my name heard in the mouth of the herald. I do not know what brought me to this land. It was like the plan of a god.'"[1]

Whatever the reason, Sinuhe fled. From the western Nile Delta, he headed south until he reached a spot where the Nile was a single stream, somewhere near modern Cairo, and crossed to the east bank. He then turned north, following the edge of cultivated land until he came to the entrance of the wadi Tumilat. This valley connects the eastern Delta with Lake Timsah, near modern Ismailia, which at the time was the starting point of a road leading through the Sinai to Edom, south of the Dead Sea, and the Negev, the vast desert in southern Canaan that is part of modern Israel. Here Amenemhat I had built a fortress, known as "The Walls of the Prince," as a barrier to infiltration by Bedouins, and Sinuhe was forced to hide in a bush so that the guard on the wall of the fortress would not see him. Once darkness had fallen, he continued his journey into the Sinai, where the chief of a Bedouin tribe gave him food and drink and helped him to reach southern Canaan. From there he continued his journey northward along the road known in the Bible as the Way of the Sea, where he was ultimately befriended by the prince Nenshi.

It is not easy to locate the precise area where Sinuhe spent his years of exile. His account of this stage of his wanderings contains the statement: "I set out for Byblos [an ancient port in northern Phoenicia] and turned to Kedem [which generally means the east]. I spent half a year there. Then Nenshi, son of Amu, the ruler of Upper Retenu, brought me [to him, Nenshi]." The mention of Byblos has been interpreted as meaning that the area where Sinuhe eventually settled is to be found somewhere to the east of that city in northern Syria, but this is completely wrong. Sinuhe's words have to be examined in the light of the sketchy geographical knowledge of western Asia possessed by Egyptians of the time.

It was only from the beginning of the Eighteenth Dynasty, in the sixteenth century BCE, that the Egyptians gained detailed information about this area. Until then, they applied the term *Retenu* generally to Canaan and Syria. However, they knew the port of Byblos because they had regular trade contact with it by sea. The biblical Way of the Land joined the Way of the Sea at Gaza, linking Egypt with western Asia, leading to northern Syria and bypassing Byblos. But because Byblos was the only location in western Asia that was well known to the Egyptians, the statement that Sinuhe "set out for Byblos" simply signifies the geographical direction of his journey and means, "I took the road that leads to Byblos." He never states that he actually reached this city. Instead, he abandoned the Way of the Sea and "turned to Kedem [east]" at some point in Upper Retenu.

During this period (the Middle Bronze Age, 2200–1550 BCE), the

Way of the Sea was crossed, at a point level with the northern section of the Dead Sea, by an east-west road connecting Jerusalem near the river Jordan with Jaffa (Joppa) on the Mediterranean.[2] It was most probably here, near the area that was the reported scene of the combat between David and Goliath, that Sinuhe turned east, as it kept him near the road leading to Egypt, the land of his birth. Certainly, Upper Retenu, where he chose to settle, can have been only the central area of northern Canaan, rather than the city-states of northern Syria, as has been suggested. The city-states were fortified, surrounded by strong walls, with villages and cultivated land outside the walls. However, the life Sinuhe describes was among a people who were seminomadic, lived in tents, and were shepherds and hunters.

As we saw earlier, after he had lived in Upper Retenu for six months, Sinuhe's presence came to the notice of Nenshi, the ruler of the territory, who saw in the exiled Egyptian courtier a useful ally, took him under his protection, and gave him favored treatment: "He placed me before his children. He married me to his eldest daughter. He made me choose from his country the choicest part of what he owned on the border with another country. It was a good land called Yaa. Figs were there as well as grapes, and more wine than water. Its honey was abundant and its olive trees numerous. On its trees were all kinds of fruits. Barley and emmer [a kind of wheat], and there was all kinds of cattle without limit. . . . Men hunted for me and laid [food] before me in addition to the catch of my hunting dogs. . . . I spent many years while my children grew into mighty men, each managing his own tribe."

Nenshi also appointed Sinuhe as commander of his army. This favoritism toward a foreigner would appear to have made local men jealous, for Sinuhe tells us:

> There came a mighty man of Retenu to challenge me at my tent. He was a champion without equal, and he had defeated all of Retenu. He said that he would fight with me, for he thought to beat me.

He plotted to plunder my cattle through the counsel of his tribe. That ruler talked with me. I said: I do not know him. I am not his friend that I might walk about freely in his camp. . . . He is jealous because he sees me carrying out your affairs. . . . If he wishes to fight let him say so. Does God not know what is predicted for him, knowing how it is?

I spent the night stretching my bow. I shot my arrows. I took out my dagger. I fixed up my weapons. When dawn broke, Retenu had come. It had incited its tribes, and had assembled the lands of half of it. It had planned this combat. He came to me where I was standing, and I placed myself near him. Every heart for me, men and women yelled. Every heart ached for me, saying: "Is there another strong man who could fight him?" He [took up] his shield, his axe and his armful of javelins. But after I had come away from his weapons, I made his remaining arrows pass me by, as one was close to the other. Then he made out a yell, for he intended to strike me, and he approached me. I shot him. My arrow struck in his neck. He cried out and fell on his nose. I felled him with his own axe. I yelled my war cry over his back. Every Asiatic roared . . . and his people mourned for him. This ruler, Nenshi, son of Amu, took me in his embrace.

The period of Sinuhe's exile began, as we saw earlier, around 1960 BCE, the last year of Amenemhat's reign. After his death, Amenemhat's eldest son, Sesostris, married his sister, Nefru, in order to inherit the throne—as was the Egyptian custom—and ruled alone for a further thirty-five years. Throughout this time, his period in exile, Sinuhe continued to long for the land of his birth. He sent repeated messages to the palace asking that he might be allowed to return to Egypt so that he could die and be buried there. Eventually his plea was granted, and he returned to spend his last years at the Egyptian court.

Sinuhe is actually a much more important figure in biblical history than this account reveals. His story is told here merely to make the point about his combat with the mighty Canaanite, echoed in the confrontation between David and Goliath. The similarities between the two accounts have been noted by many scholars, such as William Kelly Simpson: "The . . . account of the fight with the champion of Retenu has frequently been compared to the David and Goliath duel, for which it may have served as a literary prototype."[3]

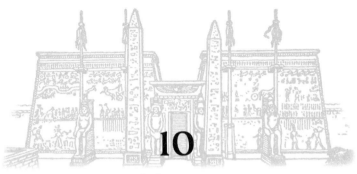

10

Joseph's Dreams

WHILE TUTHMOSIS III WAS CREATING the richest and most powerful empire the world had yet seen, Sarah and her descendants were leading a nomadic life in Canaan. Tents provided simple homes and protection against the often harsh elements. Marriages were arranged, children born, the dead buried. The rhythm of their days was set by trying to coax a living from the unpromising soil and caring for their modest herds of sheep, goats, and cattle. Nonetheless, the story of their lives at this time, as we find in Genesis, indicates that memories of those early links with the royal house of Egypt, although growing fainter with each passing year, still survived among Sarah's descendants.

When Isaac, the son of Sarah's bigamous marriage to Tuthmosis III, grew to manhood, he is said to have taken a wife, Rebekah. Like Sarah before her, Rebekah is described as infertile, but this may be simply a way of saying that, at a time when early marriage was the norm, a girl had been taken as a bride long before she reached childbearing age.

Eventually, Rebekah gave birth to twin sons. The first to be born was named Esau, the second Jacob (*Ya'qwb*, which means in Hebrew "the one who follows"). The most intriguing aspect of their early life is Esau's sale of his birthright:

Once when Jacob was cooking some stew, Esau came in from the open country, famished. He said to Jacob, "Quick, let me have some of that red stew! I'm famished!" . . . Jacob replied, "First sell me your birthright." "Look, I am about to die," Esau said. "What good is the birthright to me?" But Jacob said, "Swear to me first." So he swore an oath to him, selling his birthright to Jacob. Then Jacob gave Esau some bread and some lentil stew. . . . So Esau despised his birthright. (Genesis 25:29–34)

What was this birthright that Esau sold to Jacob? To what exactly did this birthright entitle its owner? The only logical explanation would be the inheritance of property or a title. We know from an account in the Talmud that Jacob did not receive any of Isaac's property after his father's death, but Esau gave him Isaac's promise, the empire:

Then Isaac died, and Jacob and Esau wept together for their father's demise. They carried his body to the cave of Machpelah, which is in Hebron, and all the kings of Canaan followed with the mourners in the funeral train of Isaac. . . . Isaac bequeathed his cattle and his possessions to his two sons. Esau said then to Jacob, "Behold, this which our father has left us must be divided into two portions, then I will select my share." Jacob divided all his father's possessions into two portions in the presence of Esau and his sons, and then addressing his brother, said:

"Take unto thyself both these portions which thou seest before thee. Behold, the God of Heaven and Earth spoke unto our ancestors, Abraham and Isaac, saying, 'Unto thy seed will I give this land as an everlasting possession.' Now, all that our father left is before thee; if thou desirest the promised possession, the land of Canaan, take it, and this other wealth shall be mine; or if thou desirest these two portions, be it as it is pleasing in thy eyes, and the land of

Canaan shall be the share for me and mine."...

Esau ... gave Jacob for his portion the land ... from the river of Egypt unto the great river, the river Euphrates.[1]

From this account, we can see that the birthright that passed from Esau, the elder twin, to Jacob was the princely title that flowed from the identity of their grandfather, Tuthmosis III.

While Esau did not take the promise seriously, Jacob still hoped that one day he would be able to inherit his father's legacy. As he was living in tents and leading a simple nomadic life with his flock in Canaan, he still dreamed that one day he or his descendants would inherit the vast kingdom stretching from the Nile to the Euphrates. Of the two brothers, the Old Testament suggests that Jacob would have more faith in the fulfillment of such a promise at some time in the future. We are told in Genesis 25:27 that the twin brothers had vastly different characters. Esau was "a skilful hunter, a man of the open country," but Jacob, like Joseph, the son who would be born to him, seems to have been more of a dreamer.

Later Jacob is said to have had an encounter with the Lord, which resulted in his name being changed: "Your name is Jacob, but you will no longer be called Jacob; your name will be Israel" (Genesis 35:10). As the Hebrew verb *srh* means "to be a leader" (or a commander), and *el* is the short form of *Elohim* (God), the new name means "Elohim rules."

More significant is the fact that this change of name comes just before the story of Joseph and his dreams. Like Jacob his father, although he was a younger son, Joseph shared his father's dreams about the promised inheritance and the royal connection. That is why

Israel loved Joseph more than any of his other sons ... and he made a richly ornamented robe for him. When his brothers saw that their father loved him more than any of them, they hated him. ...

Joseph had a dream, and when he told it to his brothers, they
hated him all the more. He said to them, "Listen to this dream I
had. We were binding sheaves of grain out in the field when suddenly my sheaf rose and stood upright, while your sheaves gathered
around mine and bowed down to it." His brothers said to him, "Do
you intend to reign over us? Will you actually rule us?" And they
hated him all the more because of his dream and what he had said.
(Genesis 37:3–8)

Then Joseph had a second dream, which he related to his father as
well as to his brothers: "I had another dream, and this time the sun and
the moon and eleven stars were bowing down to me" (Genesis 37:9).
This served to fuel the jealousy of his brothers, and Jacob rebuked
him, saying: "Will your mother and I and your brothers come and bow
down to the ground before you?" (Genesis 37:10).

By giving his son the ornamented robe, Jacob was passing to Joseph
his own birthright, which he had bought from his brother, Esau. This
made the young lad feel more important than his elder brothers, for
which they hated him. His brothers' revenge was to humiliate Joseph
and show him that his dream was false by selling him as a slave to
Egypt, the land of his royal dreams. They sold him to Ishmaelite traders whose caravan was on its way to the land of the Nile.

When the merchants reached their destination, they sold Joseph to
Potiphar, the captain of the pharaoh's guard, who found him a faithful servant and entrusted to him everything he owned. Joseph was not
only efficient but handsome, and after a while Potiphar's wife tried to
seduce him. When he refused to lie with her, Potiphar's wife accused
him of trying to rape her, and the lad was sent to jail.

In prison, Joseph met the pharaoh's chief cupbearer and chief
baker, who had been locked up after giving offense to the king.
When both of them had strange dreams, they asked Joseph to interpret them. Joseph predicted—accurately—that the cupbearer would

be released and restored to his position, while the baker would be hanged.

Some two years later, according to Genesis 41:1, the pharaoh himself had two mysterious dreams that none of the wise men of Egypt could interpret for him. The cupbearer explained to the pharaoh how Joseph had interpreted his and the baker's dreams and events had turned out exactly as predicted. The pharaoh sent for Joseph and said: "I had a dream, and no one can interpret it. But I have heard it said of you that when you hear a dream you can interpret it. . . . In my dream, I was standing on the bank of the Nile, when out of the river there came up seven cows, fat and sleek, and they gazed among the reeds. After them, seven other cows came up—scrawny and very ugly and lean. . . . Then the lean, ugly cows ate up the seven fat cows" (Genesis 41:15, 17–20).

The pharaoh had another dream: "In my dream I saw seven heads of grain, full and good, growing on a single stalk. After them, seven other heads sprouted—withered and thin. . . . The thin heads of grain swallowed the seven good heads. I told this to my magicians, but none of them could explain it to me" (Genesis 41:22–24).

Joseph said to the pharaoh: "The dreams of Pharaoh are one and the same. God has revealed to Pharaoh what he is about to do. The seven good cows are seven good years, and the seven good heads of grain are seven years; it is one and the same dream. The seven lean, ugly cows that came up afterwards are seven years, and so are the seven worthless heads of grain. . . . Seven years of great abundance are coming throughout the land of Egypt, but seven years of famine will follow them. . . . Now let Pharaoh look for a discerning and wise man and put him in charge of the land of Egypt" (Genesis, 41:25–27, 29–30, 33).

Seeing that Joseph was the right man for the job, the pharaoh told him: "'I hereby put you in charge of the whole land of Egypt.' Then Pharaoh took his signet ring from his finger and put it on Joseph's finger. He dressed him in fine linen and put a gold chain around his neck. He had him ride in a chariot as his second in command, and people shouted before him, 'Make way!' . . . Pharaoh gave Joseph the name Zaphenath-Paneah [Sef-net-pa-ankh] and gave him . . . [the] daughter of Potiphera, priest of On [Heliopolis], to be his wife" (Genesis 41:41–45).

Thus, according to the Bible, Joseph's dreams of becoming a ruler in Egypt were fulfilled when he was thirty years old. It will be surprising to learn the identity of the pharaoh who appointed this Hebrew to rule over Egypt.

11

The Dreamer Pharaoh

SOMETIME AFTER THE BIRTH OF ISAAC, it seems that Abraham became separated from his wife Sarah. Nevertheless, Abraham managed to get hold of the boy without his mother's knowledge and traveled to Jerusalem, intending to offer him as a sacrifice on the altar. Although Josephus, the Jewish historian of the first century CE, says that Isaac was twenty-five at the time, we do not know exactly how old the boy was when his father tried to kill him. In any case, the Bible story makes it clear that Sarah never knew that Abraham had taken her son away, nor did she know of Abraham's intention to sacrifice her son on the altar. According to a story in the Aggadah, the collection of materials in the Talmud and Mishnah containing exegesis and retellings of biblical stories, "Satan being annoyed . . . turned his attention to Sarah. He said to her 'Your husband has seized the boy, and sacrificed him. The boy wailed and wept; but he could not escape from his father.' Sarah began to cry bitterly, and ultimately died of her grief."[1]

Although Abraham was 130 years old when Sarah died, not only did he take another wife, named Keturah, but he was also able to have six sons with her. But none of his children except Isaac had any share in God's promises to their father. According to Josephus, Keturah's sons were placed in Arabia. Furthermore, according to Islamic tradition, Ishmael, although born in Canaan, also lived in Arabia. The biblical narrator does not seem to be much interested in Abraham's seven other sons and only follows the story of Isaac.

When Isaac was forty years old, Abraham sent Eliezer, his steward, into Mesopotamia to find a wife for him from his nephew Bethuel's family. Eliezer chose Rebekah, the granddaughter of Abraham's brother. After some years, Rebekah, Isaac's only wife, gave birth to his twin sons, Esau and Jacob. Abraham is said to have died at the advanced age of 175, when Isaac was seventy.

When Isaac became blind in his old age, his son Jacob had already married four women and had twelve children. Uncertain when he might die, and unaware that Esau had already sold his birthright to his brother, Isaac wanted to give his blessing to his elder son. He asked Esau to kill an animal and prepare savory meat for him, so that he could eat it and give him his blessing. His mother Rebekah, who overheard the conversation, wanted the blessing to go to her other son, Jacob. So she quickly ordered Jacob to bring her two goat kids from their flock, and she cooked the meal herself. Rebekah then dressed Jacob in the festive garments of Esau and covered his smooth neck and hands with the skins of the kids, then asked Jacob to take the meal to his father. Although he was suspicious when he heard his voice, Isaac was assured when he touched Jacob's hands, covered with animal skin, and gave him his blessing. Soon after, when Esau returned from the hunt, he prepared the venison and brought it to his father. He cried with anger when he realized what had happened.

It is significant that the importance attached to the birthright is only found in Isaac's family and disappears completely after Joseph's arrival in Egypt. This indicates that until that time, Sarah's descendants must have been aware of their royal ancestor, hoping one day to be recognized as princes of Egypt.

Joseph, the son of Jacob (who received his father Isaac's blessing), went down to Egypt, the country of his great-grandfather,

Tuthmosis III. When we try to identify the dreaming pharaoh who appointed Joseph over Egypt, we find some difficulty, caused by the inflated biblical chronology, because the Bible gives highly exaggerated figures for the ages of the patriarchs. For according to the Bible:

Abraham lived 175 years

Isaac lived 180 years

Jacob lived 147 years

This makes the total age of the three generations—Abraham, Isaac, and Jacob—502 years. When we deduct the 100 years that Abraham lived before the birth of Isaac (Genesis 21:5), the 60 years that Isaac lived before the birth of Jacob (Genesis 25:26), and the 130 years that Jacob lived before going down to Egypt, we find that Jacob, Abraham's grandson, came to Egypt 290 years after the birth of Abraham.

On the other hand, when we look at the Egyptian chronology of Tuthmosis III and his successor up to the fifth year of Merneptah, when his Israel Stele (usually dated to 1208 or 1270 BCE) mentions the Israelites as already in Canaan, we find the length of their reigns as follows:

Tuthmosis III, 54 years

Amenhotep II, 23 years

Tuthmosis IV, 8 years

Amenhotep III, 38 years

Akhenaten (alone), 6 years

Tutankhamun, 9 years

Aye, 4 years

Horemheb, 13 years

Ramses I, 12 years

Seti I, 29 years

Ramses II, 67 years

Merneptah, 5 years

Biblical chronology suggests that Joseph's appointment as an Egyptian minister took place 290 years after Isaac's birth. Egyptian chronology, on the other hand, makes the length between Isaac's birth (during Tuthmosis III's reign) and the fifth year of Merneptah (when the Israelites had settled in Canaan) only 258 years. This shows that biblical chronology cannot be trusted in historical matters, as it gives inflated ages for the patriarchs. In this case, it would be safer to rely on the more secure Egyptian chronology. The pharaoh who appointed Joseph to be one of his ministers over the land of Egypt must have been a descendant of Tuthmosis III. Assuming that the average age in Egypt and Canaan at the time was the same, we have to look for Tuthmosis III's successor, who was contemporary with Jacob, of the second generation of Abraham's descendants.

Tuthmosis III, the pharaoh who married Sarah and fathered Isaac, had many other wives, including three foreign women. As his firstborn son, Amenemhat, had died before him, the king chose another son, Amenhotep II, to be his coregent two years before he died in his year 54 (1436 BCE). Amenhotep II was the son of Merytra, daughter of Huy, whose title was Divine Adoratrice of Amun. Like his father, Amenhotep was a warrior king, who went out to crush a revolt in Syria during his early years on the throne. As a young man, Amenhotep is known for his athletic abilities: he shot arrows through a copper plate while driving a chariot with the reins tied to his vest. Like his father, Amenhotep had many wives, but the wife whose son followed him on the throne was named Tiaa. After twenty-three years of rule, Amenhotep II died and was succeeded by Tuthmosis IV (ca. 1413–1395 BCE), the eighth ruler of the Eighteenth Dynasty, and the pharaoh who appointed Joseph as his minister.

Tuthmosis IV was not his father's chosen successor to the throne. But one day, as a young prince, he went hunting in his chariot near the pyramids. At noon, when the sun was at its highest, he rested in the shadow of the Sphinx and fell asleep. The gigantic Sphinx was at that time more than half buried, with only its head visible above the sand. In his sleep, the prince had a vision in which he was addressed by Harmakhis, the sun god with whom the Sphinx was identified, who said:

> Look upon me, contemplate me, O my son Thothmos; I am father, Harmakhis-Khopri-Ra-Tumu; I bestow upon thee sovereignty over my domain, the supremacy over the living; thou shalt wear its white crown and its red crown on the throne of Seb the hereditary chief. May the earth be thine in all its length and breadth; may the splendour of the universal master illuminate (thee); may there come unto thee the abundance that is in the double land, the riches brought from every country and the long duration of years. Thine is my face, thine is my heart; thy heart is mine. Behold the actual condition that thou mayest protect all my perfect limbs. The sand of the desert whereon I am laid has covered me. Save me, causing all that is in my heart to be executed. For I know that thou my son, my avenger . . . behold I am with thee. I am [thy father].[2]

The prince took this encounter as a covenant between him and his god: he would inherit the kingdom if he cleared the sand from the Sphinx. Tuthmosis's dream was fulfilled, and he succeeded his father on the throne of Egypt. Immediately upon his accession to the throne, Tuthmosis IV hastened to fulfill his part of the covenant. In order to preserve the memory of his action, he placed a carved stone tablet, now known as the Dream Stele, between the two paws of the Sphinx.

Abraham and Sarah made their journey to Egypt when Tuthmosis III, the sixth ruler of the Eighteenth Dynasty, was on the throne. It was this pharaoh who married Sarah and fathered Isaac, the son born to her after the couple had returned to Canaan. On the death of Isaac, the elder of his twin sons, Esau, sold the birthright of his title as a prince of Egypt cheaply to the younger one, Jacob, from whom it passed to his beloved son, Joseph. It was Tuthmosis IV, the eighth king of the Eighteenth Dynasty, in residence at Memphis and ruling over the empire—from the borders of Egypt to the river Euphrates—described in the promise to Abraham about his seed, who appointed Joseph over the land of Egypt, after he had been sold into slavery and had successfully interpreted the king's dreams.

In my book *The Hebrew Pharaohs of Egypt,* I have identified biblical Joseph as Yuya, who was appointed by Tuthmosis IV to serve the king. Like Joseph, Tuthmosis IV was a dreamer whose dream was fulfilled. Although Tuthmosis IV died very young—in his mid-twenties—his son and successor Amenhotep III not only kept Joseph (Yuya) in his court but also married his daughter Tiye and made her queen over Egypt.

12

Uniting the Families of Egypt and Canaan

AMENHOTEP III, THE SON OF TUTHMOSIS IV, sat on the throne at a time when Egypt and the countries in her empire were enjoying a time of peace and prosperity. His reign was a period of unprecedented prosperity and splendor, when Egypt reached the peak of its artistic and international power. A combination of diplomacy, judicious marriages, and a liberal use of gold secured a balance of power between Egypt and its neighboring states: the Mitanni in northern Syria; the Hittites of Asia Minor; and the Assyrians and Babylonians in Mesopotamia. Canaan and Syria posed no threat, and the southern frontier was secured up to and beyond the Nile's fourth cataract.

Trade and gifts exchanged with rulers in the empire dominated Amenhotep's foreign relations. Luxuries from the Levant and the Aegean world poured into the country on a greater scale than ever before, while in Egypt itself more land was brought under cultivation, art flourished, and prosperous officials and priests enjoyed the pleasures of new townhouses and country villas with large estates. The common people also benefited from the general prosperity and from the state projects that offered alternative employment during the long summer droughts.

Amenhotep III not only kept Joseph in the official positions he had obtained during the previous reign, but he also took a significant step toward uniting the two branches of Tuthmosis III's descendants through Tuthmosis III's two wives: Sarah the Hebrew and Merytra, daughter of Huy and the Divine Adoratrice of Amun. Amenhotep was about twelve when he ascended the throne, and he had to marry Sitamun, his baby sister, in order to confirm his right to it. Although Sitamun was only two years old at the time, she was the heiress whose husband, according to Egyptian customs, would obtain the right to succeed her father.

A short time after ascending the throne, before the end of his year 2, Amenhotep also married Tiye, daughter of Yuya, whom I have identified as Joseph the patriarch. Moreover, Amenhotep decided to make Tiye his Great Royal Wife—the queen. This was against Egyptian tradition, according to which the king could marry as many women as he desired, but the queen, whose children would follow him on the throne, had to come from the heiress, daughter of the previous pharaoh.

As Sitamun was only two when Amenhotep married her, the king fell in love with Tiye, the older girl, who lived with him in the royal palace at Memphis. Tiye's mother, Tuya, was the king's "ornament" (*khrt bsw*), a post that might be said to involve the duties of a modern lady-in-waiting. This meant that she had to live in the vicinity of the royal residence. It was thus that the prince Amenhotep grew up with and fell in love with Tiye. The marriage between Amenhotep III and Tiye is attested by an issue of scarabs dated to year 2 of his reign, copies of which were also found in Palestine: "Live . . . King Amenhotep (III), who is given life, (and) the Great King's Wife Tiye, who liveth. The name of her father is Yuya, the name of her mother is Tuya. She is the wife of a mighty king whose southern boundary is as far as Karoy [in northern Sudan] and northern as far as Naharin [in northern Syria]."[1]

WIVES AND HAREMS

Along with his queens Sitamun and Tiye, Amenhotep III had a large harem, including two princesses from Babylon and two princesses from Mitanni. In his year 10, when Gilukhepa, daughter of the prince of Naharina, arrived in Egypt, she was accompanied by 317 women in her retinue, who became part of his harem.

Why did Amenhotep III insist on making Tiye his Great Royal Wife, allowing her to be portrayed sitting next to him, depicted

Amenhotep III seated beside his wife Tiye, daughter of Yuya (Joseph).
The statue is housed at the Museum of Egyptian Antiquities in Cairo.

in sculpture in equal size, for the first time in Egypt? Why did Amenhotep III allow the tribe of Israel to come down and join Joseph and his family, who were living in Egypt? Could it be that Amenhotep III became aware of the family relationship between Tiye's father (Joseph) and Tuthmosis III, his own great-grandfather?

Following his brothers' second visit to Egypt to buy food, Joseph obtained the pharaoh's permission for his father and all the members of his family to come and live in Egypt. In all, we are told that the number of Israelites who settled in Egypt as a result of this arrangement totaled seventy, although only sixty-nine are named. Since Joseph and his two sons, Manasseh and Ephraim, are mentioned by name in the biblical list, it is reasonable to conclude that the seventieth member of the tribe of Israel was already in Egypt. I believe that she was a daughter of Joseph—Tiye, Yuya's daughter, who became queen.

Nevertheless, the Israelites were shepherds. They were not allowed to settle in the Nile Valley, because shepherds had been regarded as an abomination by the Egyptians ever since the century-long occupation and rule of the eastern Delta by the pastoral Hyksos before the foundation of the Eighteenth Dynasty. Instead the Israelites were given land in Goshen, to the east of the Nile Delta, which was remote from the seat of the pharaoh's residence. Goshen was near the military border city of Zarw, at modern Qantara East, overlooking the Suez Canal.

Although Amenhotep III is known to have had his royal residence at Memphis, near present-day Saqqara, until his year 20, when he moved to his newly built residence at Malqata in western Thebes, the biblical story of Moses implies that the ruling pharaoh of the time had a residence in the vicinity of Goshen: he was in a position to give orders in person to the midwives to kill male children born to Israelite women, while the sister of Moses was able to watch his basket and see the pharaoh's daughter picking him up from the water.

It seems that the king, who wanted to allow his wife a chance to see her father's family, established a summer royal residence for her in Zarw, in the same area as the biblical Goshen. We know this from Amenhotep's pleasure-lake scarab, dated to his year 11, which indicates that the queen had a residence in this area. Six versions have been found of the scarab, which was issued to commemorate the creation of a pleasure lake for the Great Royal Wife, Tiye. Although there are some minor differences, they all agree on the main points of the text, which runs as follows:

> Year 11, third month of Inundation (first season), day 1, under the majesty of Horus . . . mighty of valour, who smites the Asiatics, King of Upper and Lower Egypt, Neb-Maat-Re, Son of Re Amenhotep Ruler of Thebes, who is given life, and the Great Royal Wife Tiye, who liveth, His Majesty commanded the making of a lake for the Great King's Wife Tiye, who liveth, in the city of Zarw-kha. Its length 3700 cubits, its breadth 700 cubits. [One of the scarabs, a copy of which is kept at the Vatican, gives the breadth as 600 cubits, and also mentions the names of the queen's parents, Yuya and Tuya, indicating that they were still alive at the time.] His Majesty celebrated the feast of the opening of the lake in the third month of the first season, day 16, when His Majesty sailed thereon in the Royal barge Aten Gleams.[2]

YUYA AND JOSEPH

John Henry Breasted, the American Egyptologist, believed that while the origin of the powerful Tiye is obscure, the persistent publication of the names of her untitled parents on different scarabs is remarkable, indicating that they could be of foreign origin.

Yuya's (Joseph's) tomb was discovered in 1905, after the American Theodore M. Davis had obtained a concession to excavate in the Valley of the Kings in Luxor, the ancient Thebes. Davis, who took to spending the winters of his old age there, provided the money while excavation work was carried out by officials of the Egyptian Service of Antiquities. The tomb was officially opened on February 13, 1905, and was attended by a brother of the king of England, the Duke of Connaught, and his duchess, who happened to be visiting Egypt at the time.

The rich tomb given to Yuya and his wife among the royalty in the Valley of the Kings suggests their importance in this reign. Until the discovery of Tutankhamun's tomb seventeen years later, Yuya's tomb was the only one to be found almost intact. Along with the two sarcophaguses of Yuya and his wife, including their mummies, the tomb contained different relics, such as:

- A chest offered by Queen Tiye, his daughter.
- A papyrus containing chapters of the Book of the Dead, including the images of seven cows in heaven.
- Three objects given to Yuya by the king, similar to those given to Joseph by the pharaoh on his appointment: a golden necklace, a chariot, and the title of "Bearer of the King's Ring."
- Three small chairs of Sitamun, made for her when she was a child, indicating that after her father's early death she was reared by Tuya. She must have been about fifteen years of age when she gave the chairs to be included in the funerary furniture, around year 13 of Amenhotep III's reign.

The different ways in which Yuya's name was written on his objects relates him to Yahweh, or Jehovah, the god of the Israelites. His name was found in his tomb spelled in different ways: *Yaa, Ya, Yu-Ya, Ya-Yi, Yu, Yu-Yu, Ya-Ya, Yi-Ay, Yi-a,* and *Yuy-y.* As we can see, in most of these cases his name is written in two syllables, *Yu* and *Ya.* Every syllable begins with the letter Y. *Yu* (or *Jo* in English) is the short name for Yahweh, the Hebrew god, and is also the first part of *Yoseph,* Joseph's name, while the second part, *seph* (*sef*), represents the first part of the Egyptian name that the pharaoh gave to Joseph

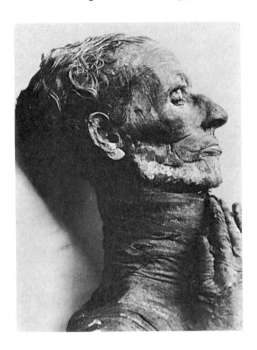

The mummy of Yuya, identified as Joseph. Joseph was appointed minister by Tuthmosis IV and remained in the royal court under Amenhotep III.

on his appointment—Zaphenath-Paneah, or Sef-net-pa-ankh, which means "God says he will live."

From the objects found in his tomb, we can see that Yuya (Joseph) held an important position in the pharaonic court of Amenhotep III. As well as holding the title "Holy Father of the Lord of the Two Lands," which he received after the king married his daughter, he was also "Master of the Horses," "Deputy of His Majesty in the Chariotry," "Bearer of the Ring of the King of Lower Egypt," "Seal-Bearer of the King of Lower Egypt," "Hereditary Noble and Count," "Favorite of the Good God (Pharaoh)," "Ears of the King of Lower Egypt," "Sole Friend," "Great Prince," "Beloved of the King of Upper Egypt," "Beloved of the King of Lower Egypt," "Praised of the Lord Amun," "First among the King's Companions," and "The Wise One."

His mummy, one of the best examples of Egyptian mummification, looks very impressive, which persuaded the British Egyptologist Arthur Weigall to comment in his book *The Life and Times of Akhnaton* [sic: *Akhenaten*], published in 1910:

He was a person of commanding presence, whose powerful character showed itself in his face. One must picture him now as a tall man, with a fine shock of white hair, a great hooked nose like that of a Syrian; full, strong lips; and a prominent, determined jaw. He has the face of an ecclesiastic, and there is something about his mouth which reminds one of the late Pope, Leo XIII. One feels on looking at his well-preserved features, that there may be found the originator of the great religious movement which his daughter and grandson [Queen Tiye and Akhenaten, her son] carried into execution.[3]

A short time after her marriage, Tiye gave birth to her first son, Tuthmosis, who lived with his parents at the royal residence in Memphis, where he was educated and trained by the priests. But after the king his father appointed him as the high priest of Ptah, a position held by the heir apparent during the Eighteenth Dynasty, he suddenly and mysteriously disappeared from the scene, certainly at the hands of Amun's priests. That is why, when the queen became pregnant again in Amenhotep III's year 11, the king feared that if she gave birth to a boy, he might have another confrontation with the priests. It also explains why Tiye kept her new son, later named Akhenaten, away from the royal residence, out of fear for his life.

AMENHOTEP'S ADMINISTRATION

In order to be able to manage the affairs of a large empire, Amenhotep needed a large and efficient administration. Growing wealth presented new problems in administration for the Egyptians. With the extensive wealth and land of the Egyptian empire at the accession of Amenhotep III, the new pharaoh had to have an army of officials to see to the growing kingdom. These administrators followed him when he moved his residence from Memphis to Thebes, so that the king would be surrounded by chosen, loyal, dedicated, and competent officials. At the same time, the majority of officials in his reign were given their titles through family inheritance, as was the tradition of the time, while many of the lesser positions were given to people of humble background. These chosen officials were of extreme importance throughout the reign of Amenhotep, as they contributed to the immense building programs, the day-to-day issues that arose in Egypt, trade, and the duty of keeping the peace with the neighboring nations.

Amenhotep III's reign, which lasted nearly forty years, was both stable and prosperous, more as a result of international trade and a strong supply of gold than of conquest and expansion. Due to his country's prosperity in a time of peace, Amenhotep was able to become a great builder. Throughout the country, new temples were founded and old ones restored. One of the biggest projects was Amenhotep's splendid palace, the Malqata, in western Thebes, opposite modern Luxor, where he moved in his year 20. This huge estate included small chapels, large audience halls, parade grounds, villas for public officials, kitchens, offices, workshops, and quarters for servants. Next to the Malqata, the king built his imposing mortuary temple. Thebes was also the seat of the state god, Amun, and here his cult received such favorable royal treatment—generous endowment for the great temple of Karnak at Thebes, gifts of land and gold—that it virtually became an arm of the state.

One of Amenhotep's greatest achievements was the temple of Amun, a large complex on the east bank of the Nile at Thebes (modern-day Luxor), including the famous reliefs on the east side, among them a scene that depicts his birth directly from the god Amun.

Amenhotep III ruled for about thirty-nine years. Shortly before his death the king became seriously ill, and the Egyptian priests, with their magic, failed to cure him. In Amenhotep's year 35 (1371 BCE), his father-in-law, Tushratta, the Hurrian king of Mitanni in northern Syria, decided to send an image of the goddess Ishtar to the pharaoh, hoping she might save his life. While the image was on its way to Egypt, Tushratta sent a letter to the king: "To Nimmu Aria (Amenhotep III), king of Egypt whom I love and who loves me. . . . Thus, speaks Shaushka (Ishtar) of Nineveh, Lady, of all the lands: I wish to go to Egypt. . . . Now I am sending you this letter and she is on the way. . . . May Shaushka, Lady of the Heavens, protect us, my brother and myself."[4]

Amenhotep III's mummy was found in the western Valley of the Kings in Luxor. He was originally buried in tomb KV 22, but his mummy was moved to chamber KV 35, where it was found in 1898 by Victor Loret. A modern CT scan has shown that the king had a degenerated spinal condition called diffuse idiopathic skeletal hyperostosis (DISH). There are also depictions of him in his final days as being visibly weak and having a sick figure. Scientists believe he was obese. Toward the end of his life he suffered severe dental problems, as can be seen in his mummy, where his teeth were found to be badly worn and his gums riddled with abscesses.

Examination of his mummy suggests that the king was about fifty when he died. As he ruled for a full thirty-eight years and died at the start of the thirty-ninth, he could have been around twelve when he came to the throne and about fourteen when he married Tiye in or just before his second regnal year.

Being the great-grandson of Tuthmosis III (the king who married Abraham's wife Sarah and fathered Isaac, her only son), Amenhotep III, knowingly or not, was able to reunite the descendants of Tuthmosis III from Egypt and Canaan. This resulted in a new age, in which the Amarna kings ruled Egypt and created the first great religious renaissance.

13

The Empire of
the King of Peace

AS WE HAVE SEEN, the pharaoh who married Sarah and fathered Isaac was Tuthmosis III, who established the great empire between the Nile and the Euphrates. Although the Bible says that this empire was ruled by King Solomon, historical evidence shows that it was Amenhotep III, the king who married Joseph's daughter, who eventually inherited the empire. In this case, I believe, both sources are right, because Solomon and Amenhotep III were one and the same person.

The task of identifying the historical Solomon is complicated not only by biblical red herrings, but by the fact that we have no historical records of a king of that name who ruled an empire. It is only when we match the details of the Old Testament account of Solomon's exploits with those of Amenhotep III that it becomes clear we are dealing with the same person.

Other than a minor military operation in northern Sudan during his year 5 (ca. 1401 BCE), Amenhotep III's reign was almost entirely peaceful. He was the first ruler of the Egyptian empire who did not launch any military campaigns in western Asia. Instead he relied on alliances and exchanges of gifts and diplomatic letters between himself and other leaders of the then-known world in order to create a climate of international friendship. He also furthered the cause of peace by a series of diplomatic marriages.

Similarly, the possession of a large and secure empire and freedom from warfare are said to have enabled Solomon to embark on a large number of projects and administrative reforms. According to Otto Eissfeldt, the German biblical scholar, there were five characteristic features of Solomon's reign:

1. Change in his kingdom's military organization and the introduction of chariotry as an essential arm of war
2. The creation of new administrative districts
3. Changes in the taxation system
4. The refinement of court procedure and maintenance of diplomatic relations with foreign courts
5. Building activity on a large scale, including the royal palace and its adjoining temple, and fortified barracks for his garrisons in the north

All of these features, as well as changes to the size of the empire, can be related to the life and times of Amenhotep III, as I shall show.

MILITARY ORGANIZATION

Tuthmosis III, who founded the great empire in the fifteenth century BCE, did have a strong, well-trained, well-organized army equipped with the best chariots of his age; otherwise he would not have been able to establish his extended empire. However, the American Egyptologist Alan Richard Schulman has shown that the chariots formed only a part of the army at the time. It was not until the early part of the reign of Amenhotep III that the chariotry became established as a separate entity from the infantry, with Yuya (Joseph) being the first minister to bear the title "Deputy of His Majesty in the Chariotry." Thus, it was Amenhotep III who organized the chariotry as a separate unit of warfare.

ADMINISTRATIVE SYSTEM AND TAXATION

Up to the time of Solomon, the structure of the administrative system in Israel was tribal, according to the Bible. It was Solomon who did away with tribal divisions and united Israel, together with other parts of the empire, into one political entity: "Solomon had twelve district governors over all Israel, who supplied provisions for the king and the royal household. Each had to provide supplies for one month of the year" (1 Kings 4:7). If we examine the matter closely, we find that this administrative system belongs not to Israel but to the Egyptian empire.

From as early as 3000 BCE, the Egyptian administration controlled the activities of the Two Lands of Egypt. It organized the royal court as well as the economy in the name of the king, the official owner of all the land. Palace officials were responsible for each administrative region, and each region had another high official with a local bureaucracy under his control. During the empire—particularly after the time of Tuthmosis III—the administrative system was reorganized to suit the needs of the age, and this system was further developed by Amenhotep III. It was then that, for the purpose of taxation, the empire was arranged in twelve administrative sections, an arrangement that the biblical narrator drew on for his account of the king whom the world now knows as Solomon.

According to Eissfeldt, almost all scholars agree that the taxation system that the Bible says was introduced by Solomon precisely matches the system that was used in Egypt after Tuthmosis III had established the new Egyptian empire. Each of the twelve areas was the responsibility of a high official and was expected to contribute sufficient tax to the country's needs for one month of the year.[1]

Coping with the administrative burdens of a vast empire required a highly developed administration. The sudden appearance of such an administration in Israelite tribal society during the "United Monarchy" of David and Solomon in the tenth century BCE, without any roots in the nation's previous history and followed by its sudden disappearance after Solomon's death, has been a source of puzzlement to scholars. The apparent contradiction is resolved, however, once identification of the historical David as Tuthmosis III and Solomon as Amenhotep III makes it clear that the sophisticated administration described in the Old Testament is the one established by these two monarchs in the fifteenth and fourteenth centuries BCE to deal with the task of ruling Egypt and its empire.

COURT OFFICIALS

We find among the list of Solomon's officials the priests, the scribes, the commander-in-chief of the army, the official in charge of the palace, and another in charge of the tribute. All of these new offices, not known before in Israel, are similar to appointments made by Amenhotep III. Even the forced labor pressed into service in Egypt for the king's building projects is said to have been imposed for the first time by Solomon on native Israelites as well as foreigners: "King Solomon conscripted laborers from all Israel—thirty thousand men" (1 Kings 5:13). A figure of 550 officials simply to supervise labor is given in 1 Kings 9:23.

EMPIRE IN FLUX

According to the Bible, the empire inherited by Solomon was weakened during the course of his reign. The king faced troubles in Edom, while his influence in Syria was also weakened when Rezon is said to have seized Damascus and made himself king there. These rebellions find their echo in the Amarna letters, the foreign archives of the Eighteenth Dynasty relating to the reign of Amenhotep III. Frederick J. Giles, the Canadian Egyptologist who made a study of them, came to the conclusion that "most of the letters that deal with the alleged collapse of the Egyptian empire during the Amarna period" come from the period of his rule.[2] Thus the biblical account of changes in David's empire during the time of Solomon can be seen to accord with events during the reign of Amenhotep III.

Letters sent by Canaanite kings, especially Abdi-khiba of Jerusalem, speak of continuous trouble in the area of Edom and southern Canaan: "All the king's land is rebellious." These problems in southern Canaan were not so serious that they weakened the king's control in the area, but the situation in northern Syria was far more critical. Even before Amenhotep III came to the throne, the northern Mesopotamian kingdom of Mitanni, defeated by Tuthmosis III, had begun to reassert its influence over city-states in northern Syria. Amenhotep III responded to this threat with a peace treaty with the king of Mitanni and marriage to two Mitannian princesses. He also sent the king of Mitanni thirty units of gold each year in return for his protecting the northern Syrian section of the empire.

However, Amenhotep III's problems in the region were not yet over. Toward the end of his reign, the king's authority over the northern part of the empire, including Damascus, was endangered by the powerful Hittite king Suppiluliuma I. The Hittites were an Asiatic people who settled in Anatolia in the third millennium BCE. They also posed a threat to Mitanni, Egypt's ally in the area. Akizzi, ruler of the northern Syrian city of Qatna, a few miles north of Qadesh, spoke of these dangers in letters to Amenhotep III: "To King Annumuria (Amenhotep III), Son of the Sun, my Lord thus [says] this thy servant Akizzi . . . the King of the Hittites . . . sends forth . . . as for me, I am with the King, and with the land of Egypt."[3]

Despite trouble in some regions, both Amenhotep III and Solomon were not concerned with military might and conquest but rather with rebuilding and enhancing the regions they ruled. According to the Bible, Solomon, whose period is called the Golden Age of Israelite history, is known for his building exploits: "Here is the account of the forced labor King Solomon conscripted to build the LORD's temple. His own palace, the supporting terraces, the wall of Jerusalem, and Hazor, Megiddo and Gezer. . . . He built up Lower Beth Horon, Baalath, and Tadmor in the desert within his land, as well as all his store cities and the towns for his chariots and for his horses—whatever he desired to build in Jerusalem, in *Lebanon* and throughout all the territory he ruled" (1 Kings 9:15, 17–19; emphasis added). Further reference to this mass of building work, including "store cities," which Solomon built in Hamath, is to be found in 2 Chronicles 8:3–6. Lebanon, which is included in Solomon's empire, was among the nations conquered by David according to the biblical account, and it was part of Tuthmosis III's empire.

The Bible mentions Hazor, Megiddo, and Gezer in connection with Solomon. Again, we find that all of these were among the western Asiatic cities conquered by Tuthmosis III in the middle of the fifteenth century BCE. This has been confirmed by archaeological digs, which have produced evidence of each city's destruction in the strata corresponding to his period. In addition, in all three cases, evidence has been found of large-scale reconstruction work half a century later, during the reign of Amenhotep III. New royal palaces, temples, ordinary houses, and fortifying walls were established. Like Amenhotep III, Solomon was known for his massive building projects. In the time of Amenhotep III, in each of the reconstructed cities a local ruler was appointed, paying tribute to the pharaoh and enjoying the support of an Egyptian garrison. Egyptian objects, including a cartouche of Amenhotep III, were found in the strata belonging to this period, as is the case in other excavated cities of Canaan such as Beth She'an and Lachish. Evidence of the cities' wealth and trade was found. It was clearly in this period—during the fourteenth century BCE—that these cities prospered.

KING OF PEACE

According to the Bible, Solomon was not the original name of the son of David and Bathsheba: "Because the LORD loved him, he sent word through Nathan the prophet to name him Jedidiah" (2 Samuel 12:25; *Jedidiah* means "loved by the Lord"). The name *Solomon* is derived from the Semitic *salam,* or Hebrew *shalom,* which means "peace." *Solomon* in this case seems to be a title rather than a name. It is not known if this name was used for him at the time of his reign. This could be why, although he ruled over a great empire, no historical evidence has ever been found of a king named Solomon. Rather than looking for a name, we have to find a king who ruled an empire between Egypt and the Euphrates in peace. Here we find only one king, Amenhotep III, the ninth king of the Egyptian Eighteenth Dynasty, who inherited the empire of his great-grandfather, Tuthmosis III.

Amenhotep III's reign was almost entirely peaceful. Because of his peaceful activity in Canaan, the holy city of the Jebusites, where Tuthmosis III had spent seven months with the Ark of Amun, this city was named Yerushalayim, or Jerusalem, the city of peace. We will talk more about Jerusalem and the Temple later and will show the relation Amenhotep III had to the City of David.

Among the historical records of Tuthmosis III found at Karnak is a list of more than a thousand names of Canaanite locations that fell under Egyptian control after his first Asiatic campaign. At the top of this list we find the name Qadesh. Because it is included in a list of cities in Canaan, it could not have been the Syrian city of that name. As we saw in chapter 4, it is likely that it refers to Jerusalem, which was evidently known as Qadesh, the "holy city," from ancient times. This can explain why, although Tuthmosis III had conquered the whole land of Canaan, the name *Jerusalem* does not appear in his western Asiatic city list, or in the lists of any of his immediate successors.

However, about a hundred years later, during the time of Amenhotep III, we find a new name for the city, provided by the Tell el-Amarna letters, the foreign archives of the Eighteenth Dynasty. Six communications sent to the king of Egypt in the fourteenth century BCE and written in Akkadian, the diplomatic language of the period, come from *mat Urusalim,* "the land of Jerusalem." The letters confirm that this city had been under Egyptian control since the time of Tuthmosis III, with an Egyptian military garrison stationed locally.

Furthermore, the Akkadian name for Jerusalem, found in the Amarna letters, can be divided into two elements, *uru* and *salim.* The first element, *uru,* is derived from the verb *yara,* meaning "to found" or "to establish." The second element has caused some misunderstanding. A number of scholars have argued that it refers to a Western Semitic or Amorite god, Shulmannu or Shalim. By this view, *Urusalim* would mean "Shalim has founded." But no textual or archaeological evidence has ever been found to indicate that the Amorite god Shalim was worshipped at Jerusalem.

When we abandon this unsupported explanation, we find that *salim* was correctly understood by the Jewish rabbis in the Aggadah, the legendary part of the Talmud. *Salim* means "peace" (Hebrew *shalom* and Arabic *salam*). Thus the meaning of *Urusalim* would be "foundation of peace" or "establishing peace," an interpretation that is supported by the historical evidence: the lack of any mention of Urusalim in Egyptian sources before the Tell el-Amarna letters; the fact that Qadesh, whose name is used both in the Bible and in later Arabic texts as a synonym for *Jerusalem,* is mentioned in the lists of subdued Asiatic cities of this period; and the fact that the Qadesh in question cannot have been the city of that name on the river Orontes.

This indicates that the Canaanite holy city of Qadesh became known as Jerusalem only during the time of Amenhotep III, the king of peace. To further the cause of peace, both Amenhotep III and Solomon saw judicious marriages as an act of diplomacy.

THE PHARAOH'S DAUGHTER

One of Solomon's reported marriages, however, has been subject to much dispute. The Bible states that he married the pharaoh's daughter, receiving the city of Gezer as dowry, but it does not mention the name of this pharaoh. Many Egyptologists and biblical scholars have doubted this account. Egyptian pharaohs were known to refuse to marry their daughters to any foreigners. Scholar Paul S. Ash writes: "From what is currently known, reigning Pharaohs did not marry their daughters to foreigners. According to Kadash-Enlil I of Babylon, Amenhotep III had said, 'From of old, a daughter of the king of the land of Egypt was not given to anyone.' In addition, some evidence in Herodotus suggests that it was unusual for a Pharaoh's daughter to marry a foreigner. According to Herodotus 3.1, Cambyses of Persia attacked Egypt because Pharaoh Amasis refused to give his daughter to Cambyses."[4]

Furthermore, the Bible states that the unnamed pharaoh took possession of the Canaanite city of Gezer and gave it to Solomon: "Pharaoh king of Egypt had attacked and captured Gezer. He had set it on fire. He killed its Canaanite inhabitants and then gave it as a wedding gift to his daughter, Solomon's wife. And Solomon rebuilt Gezer" (1 Kings 9:16–17).

However, this account does not agree with historical records. Gezer, in the foothills of the Judean mountains, midway between Jerusalem and Tel Aviv, is first mentioned in the Egyptian texts of Tuthmosis III after he had captured it in approximately 1468 BCE.

Although the city faced some invasion attempts during the time of Amenhotep III's successor, Akhenaten, Gezer remained under Egyptian domination at least until the end of the thirteenth century BCE. In one of the Amarna letters, the ruler of Gezer writes to the pharaoh complaining of an attack on the city by a people, the Habiru, who are believed to be Hebrews: "So to the king my lord, my Sun; Message of Milkilu, your servant, . . . my lord, save his land from the power of the 'Apiru'" (letter no. EA271).[5] Later, during the time of Merneptah, Ramses II's successor, toward the end of the thirteenth century BCE, Gezer has apparently been recaptured. The Israelite Stele, dating from this time, says: "Canaan is captive with all woe. Ashk ɔn is conquered, Gezer seized, Yanoam made non-existent."[6]

THE BURNING OF GEZER

Canaan remained firmly under Egyptian control when Ramses III (ca. 1182–51 BCE), the second ruler of Egypt's Twentieth Dynasty, came to the throne. A papyrus found in Thebes—known as the Papyrus Harris, now in the British Museum—relates that at this comparatively late date, Ramses III built a temple of Amun in the land of Canaan, and the "foreigners of Retenu come to it, bearing their tributes before it." Furthermore, an ivory model pen case, found at the Canaanite city of Megiddo and belonging to an Egyptian envoy to foreign countries, bears the name of Ramses III.[7]

However, after the reign of Ramses III, Egypt lost control over Canaan as a result of a mass invasion by the Sea Peoples, who attacked the whole eastern Mediterranean coast from Anatolia in the north to Egypt in the south. This invasion began around 1174 BCE—year 8 of Ramses III (about the same time that, according to Greek historians, the Trojan War was taking place). The story of the invasion is recorded in the best-preserved inscriptions and reliefs on the walls of Ramses III's funerary temple in western Thebes.

Although Ramses III was able to repulse the attack on Egypt, the Hittite empire of Asia Minor was swept away, and the Hittite capital, Hattushash, burned to the ground. Nevertheless, there is textual and archaeological evidence to show that Egypt's control over Canaan continued until the middle of the twelfth century BCE, when Egypt completely lost control of all the countries of the Levant.

From then onward, archaeological features show that Gezer was inhabited by a part of the Sea Peoples, the Peleset. These were the original Philistines, who later gave their name to the land of Canaan: Palestine. As we saw in chapter 3, the archaeological evidence for this claim consists of numerous specimens of a class of painted Philistine pottery that have been recovered in southwest Canaan dating from the first half of the twelfth century BCE. Although this pottery resembles Mycenaean pottery in style, chemical and physical analyses indicate that it was made locally.

Another indication of Philistine settlement in southwest Canaan is the discovery of weapons and tools of iron—unknown to the Canaanites at the time—that can be dated to the twelfth century BCE: "It was in the second half of the twelfth century BCE that the Philistines really established themselves by building older towns and founding new ones, often no doubt in close association with the Canaanite population they now ruled."[8]

According to the Bible, although Gezer was under Philistine rule when Solomon sat on the throne (conventionally dated to ca. 965–925 BCE), it was conquered and burned by an Egyptian pharaoh, who then gave it to Solomon. We have no external sources to confirm this account. Nevertheless, the British Egyptologist Kenneth Kitchen agrees with the biblical story and believes that Siamun, the sixth king of the Twenty-First Dynasty, who ruled 986–967 BCE, was the unnamed pharaoh of the Bible who conquered Gezer. I do not take Kitchen's view seriously because, during my visit to his office at Liverpool University, he told me that if a biblical text disagrees with an Egyptian text, he would regard the biblical text as more accurate. He also told me, "The absence of evidence is not evidence," meaning that he would accept the accuracy of the biblical account without other historical evidence, or even against other evidence.

The biblical account tells us that the pharaoh who married his daughter to Solomon captured Gezer and gave it to her as a wedding present (1 Kings 9:16). But the Bible gives us no indication of exactly when this event took place, nor does it give the name of the pharaoh who led the campaign against Gezer at the time conventionally assigned to the rule of Solomon. None of the kings of the weak Twenty-First Dynasty (which, according to the accepted evidence, came to an end in 945 BCE) are known to have been involved in military campaigns in western Asia. Furthermore, Gezer, in the Judean highland some thirty kilometers west of Jerusalem, is known to have been part of the Philistine territory during this period.

Kitchen's views about Siamun's capture of Gezer have been challenged by some scholars, such as Paul S. Ash and Mark W. Chavalas. The Belgian biblical scholar Edward Lipinski contends, "The attempt at relating the destruction of Gezer to the hypothetical relationship between Siamun and Solomon cannot be justified factually, since Siamun's death preceded Solomon's accession."[9]

ROYAL MARRIAGES

The biblical account of Solomon's wives completely disagrees with what we would expect of an Israelite ruler. But it does correspond to what we know about Amenhotep III. It was he who married Sitamun (the daughter of Pharaoh Tuthmosis IV), then Tiye (daughter of Yuya—Joseph), and seven other foreign princesses. To further the cause of peace with different nations of the empire, he had a series of judicious marriages to foreign princesses: two from Syria, two from Mitanni, and two from Babylonia, as well as a princess from Arzawa in southwestern Asia Minor. As for his harem, Gilukhepa, one of his Mitannian wives, is said to have arrived in Egypt with a caravan that included 317 ladies-in-waiting. This agrees completely with the biblical account of Solomon.

Had Solomon been king of Israel, we would expect him to have had an Israelite wife to bear his successor, especially because, according to Israelite tradition, the line of descent goes through the mother. As we have seen, Sarah gave birth to Isaac from the pharaoh, not from Abraham, her husband; for this reason, it was Isaac who inherited the promise of an empire. Even today, if a Jewish man marries a Gentile woman, his children from this woman would not be regarded as Jews.

Yet all we find in the Bible story are Solomon's foreign wives, beginning with the pharaoh's daughter. According to the Bible, "King Solomon . . . loved many foreign women besides Pharaoh's daughter— Moabites, Ammonites, Edomites, Sidonians and Hittites. . . . He had seven hundred wives . . . and three hundred concubines" (1 Kings 11:1, 3). Even Rehoboam, his son who succeeded him on the throne, is said to have been the son of Naamah the Ammonite (1 Kings 14:21). Yet Solomon's marriages to foreign women were regarded as defiance against God as well as against Israelite beliefs. The Lord had instructed the Israelites, "You must not intermarry with them [foreign nations], because they will surely turn your heart after their gods" (1 Kings 11:2; cf. Exodus 34:16).

The Lord's warning proved to be right, for shortly afterward we are told that "as Solomon grew old, his wives turned his heart after other gods: and his heart was not fully devoted to the LORD his God, as the heart of David his father had been. He followed Ashtoreth [Ishtar], the goddess of the Sidonians" (1 Kings 11:4–5). This sequence of events can hardly ask for greater confirmation than we find in the historical account of Amenhotep III.

SOLOMON'S GODS

Traditionally a pharaoh was the head of all Egyptian deities and was regarded as the embodiment of the gods on Earth. He was expected to uphold *maat* (truth, harmony, justice) within his kingdom and respect all gods of the country. Although the cult of Amun was regarded as the state religion during the Eighteenth Dynasty, the pharaoh still had obligations toward all the other gods. However, near the end of his reign, Amenhotep III seems to have adopted the monotheistic god Aten, introduced by his son, Akhenaten. This can be seen from the name he gave to his youngest daughter, Beketaten, as well as some of the art of his reign:

> The deified Amenhotep III's new role as the living manifestation of all deity, including the creator/sun god Amun-Ra, was expressed in a new art style that emphasized his idealized, divine nature. Akhenaten's role as the firstborn of the creator god Shu was expressed in a new art style that emphasized his physical characteristics as Shu and his inherent female twin, Tefnut, a role also shared by Nefertiti. After Amenhotep III's first jubilee and by Akhenaten's year 3 [of the coregency], the living [god] Ra-Horakhty's names were enclosed in the cartouches of a king, and the new god appeared with full royal titulary as the rayed disk with multiple hands, in every respect the senior coregent of Akhenaten.
>
> By Akhenaten's year 5 [of the coregency], he and the Aten celebrated a jubilee of their own, after (or during) which he changed his name from Amenhotep IV to Akhenaten and dedicated the site of the "Horizon of the Aten" (Akhenaten, modern Amarna) as the chief cult center of the Aten.[10]

ANOINTING AND CORONATION

Even the account of Solomon's coronation agrees with Egyptian pharaonic tradition. According to the Bible, David ordered Solomon to be anointed "king over Israel" (1 Kings 1:34). Anointing the king at the time of his coronation was an Egyptian, not a Canaanite, custom. Although 1 Samuel says that it was adopted in the case of both Saul and David, the very Hebrew word used, *mesheh,* "to anoint," is borrowed from the Egyptian *meseh.*

While the title *Messeh* or *Messiah* now refers to Jesus Christ the redeemer, every Egyptian king had received this title at the time of his coronation. The title *Messeh* was written in hieroglyphics with the image of two crocodiles. The word for "crocodile" is pronounced *meseh.* Along with other oils and perfumes, the priests also used the fat of the crocodile to anoint the king, believing that this would give him sexual strength as well as strong descendants.

According to the Bible, King David gave his orders: "Take your lord's servants with you and set Solomon my son on my own mule. . . . Have Zadok the priest and Nathan the prophet anoint him king over Israel. Blow the trumpet and shout, 'Long live King Solomon.' Then you are to go up with him, and he is to come and sit on my throne" (1 Kings 1:33–35).

Then, we are told, "the king made a great throne covered with ivory and overlaid with fine gold. The throne has six steps, and its back had a rounded top. On both sides of the seat were armrests, with a lion standing beside each of them. Twelve lions stood on the six steps, one at either end of each step" (1 Kings 10:18–20).

Otto Eissfeldt noticed the similarity to pharaonic practice here: "It is comparatively easy to visualize the throne of gold and ivory with its six steps which stood in the audience chamber as it is described in 1 Kings. . . . The lavish use of gold can be compared without hesitation with the wonderfully-preserved chair of Tutankhamun."[11] Other aspects of the account of Solomon's coronation in 1 Kings—trumpet blowing, the acclamation "Long live King Solomon," and following the king in procession—also accord with Egyptian custom.

The similarity of Solomon's coronation with the pharaonic system goes beyond rituals. The very idea of kingship, originally foreign to the Hebrews, was accorded a place in Israelite theology similar to that in Egypt in the biblical books relating to the time of David onward:

"Some scholars argue that, in adopting the institution of kingship, Israel also adopted a pagan theory of kingship and a ritual pattern for expressing it, allegedly common to all her neighbors. In this view the king was regarded as a divine or semi-divine being."[12] This situation had nothing to do with Saul, because he was merely a head of the tribal coalition, but applied mainly to David and Solomon. In both cases, as in the Egyptian tradition, the king was regarded as the son of the deity. "You are my son; today I have become your father," Yahweh tells King David in Psalm 2:7. He also says of Solomon: "I will be his father, and he will be my son" (2 Samuel 7:14). The Israelite Lord now also refers to his kingly son as his "anointed" (Psalms 2:2; 18:50; 20:6).

The ancient idea of monarchy was built on the divine right of the king and his descendants to rule and be obeyed. Ancient kings were regarded as demigods, descended from the gods. This concept is completely out of accordance with ancient Israelite belief. The Israelite idea of a chosen people did not imply this view. Jacob and his descendants had a covenant with God to follow him, with the promise that he would make them victorious. No single man or dynasty in this tribal society was regarded as having the right to rule. For the Israelites to accept David and Solomon as sons of God, possessing this right, was a new departure for them.

The biblical account does not fit in with the life of an Israelite king of the tenth century BCE. How could the king of Israel choose all his wives from among foreign nations, without even one Israelite to bear his successor? How could Solomon, who established the Temple of Jerusalem as the house of Yahweh, disobey his God and worship other deities? These details make more sense if they are applied to Amenhotep III.

14

The "Lost" Mines
of Solomon

FIFTEEN YEARS BEFORE THE END of the nineteenth century, more
details about King Solomon came forward, neither from the Bible nor
from any historical source, but from a work of fiction. *King Solomon's
Mines,* a novel by H. Rider Haggard, the English Victorian adventure
writer, was published in 1885. Relying on the discovery in the 1870s of
an immense set of mining ruins in southern Africa—known as Great
Zimbabwe—Haggard claimed that Solomon had had great mines that
were subsequently lost to history.

As soon as the book came out, it became an immediate bestseller and
has been republished to this day. Although this was fiction, Solomon's
mines entered popular belief and were described in many books, movies,
and TV series. One point that made Haggard's claim more acceptable is
the biblical account of Ophir, a port region famous for its wealth. Both
the books of Kings and Chronicles tell of a joint expedition to Ophir by
King Solomon and the Tyrian king Hiram I from Ezion-Geber, a port
on the northern extremity of the Gulf of Aqaba in the Red Sea, which
brought back large amounts of gold, precious stone, and wood.

Although the Bible mentions the wealth that came from Ophir, it
does not say where it was located, only saying that those who journeyed

to Ophir were away for three years. Ptolemy, the Alexandrian geographer of the second century CE, placed Ophir in the Malay peninsula. Christopher Columbus believed he had found it in Haiti; others suggested India, Madagascar, Sri Lanka, Arabia, or Peru.

Were Solomon's mines just a fiction, a symbol of his wealth and wisdom, or did the story point to real, historical mines?

THE TIMNA VALLEY

After the establishment of the state of Israel in 1948, the search for Solomon's mines took another direction. Rather than looking for the king's mines far away in Africa and Asia, the search came home to Israel.

In 1959 excavations in the Arabah valley, about forty kilometers north of the Gulf of Aqaba, were carried out under Beno Rothenberg by the Arabah Expedition, with the Ha'aretz Museum in Tel Aviv and, for several years, the University of Tel Aviv. A large section of the valley, containing ancient remains of worship and copper mining, is now encompassed in a recreation park.

During the survey, it became apparent to the excavators that the Timna Valley was a major center of copper mining and processing over a period of almost six thousand years. Situated between Egypt, the Negev, and Arabia, the copper mines in the Timna Valley were probably, during this early period, part of the kingdom of Edom and worked by the Edomites. Consequently:

> By 1964, the conclusion of the initial archaeological-metallurgical investigations, it had become clear that systematic excavations at Timna would . . . assist accurate dating of the ancient industrial enterprises discovered during the surface survey. It had also become obvious that the ancient remains previously called "King Solomon's Mines" belonged in fact to several widely separated periods of activity, from the fourth millennium BCE to medieval and later times, but not

including the period of Solomon. The accurate dating of these sites had therefore become of great importance and urgency for the history of metal and they also contribute to a reliable dating of contemporary civilizations in Arabia and Edom, the Negev, the Arabah and Sinai.[1]

Although the mines in the Timna Valley, north of the Israeli port of Eilat, proved to be historical fact, not fiction, they did not belong to the time of the biblical King Solomon, but to that of the pharaohs of Egypt. Although the exact date when the Egyptians first appeared in Timna remains unrecorded, after the time of Tuthmosis III, the Timna area became part of his Egyptian empire. After that, Egypt controlled the "King's Highway" through Moab, Edom, and the Sinai. This would have given Egypt de facto control over the Timna copper mines, even if the empire's soldiers and priests did not arrive in significant numbers until after the Amarna era, in the second half of the fourteenth century BCE.

During the New Kingdom of Egypt, and until the middle of the twelfth century BCE when Egypt withdrew from its colonies in the east, the whole region was under the control of the Pharaohs of the 19th-20th Dynasties who sent mining expeditions to the Timna Valley and the Nahal (wadi) Amram south of it. After these activities came to a standstill in the twelfth century the Egyptians returned for a short while to Timna during the 22nd Dynasty, in the tenth century BCE. Mining activities were again revived at the time of the Imperial Roman occupation of the Southern Arabah and continued, with varying intensity, during the Early Islamic occupation of the area. At a very reduced scale these activities seem to have gone on until medieval times.[2]

This archaeological report agrees with what we know about this area from historical sources. After the fifteenth century BCE, Edom and the lands south of the Dead Sea came under Egyptian control as part of the empire inherited by Amenhotep III. Later, in the second half of the fourteenth century BCE, Egyptian-Midianite copper production began at Timna. A very advanced smelting furnace, consisting of a bowl-shaped smelting hearth dug into the ground and lined with clay smelting mortar, was in use.

THE HATHOR TEMPLE

Along with the mines, Rothenberg made an important new discovery in 1969. At the foot of the huge sandstone formation in the center of the Timna Valley known as King Solomon's Pillars, a small Egyptian temple was excavated. The temple, dedicated to Hathor, the Egyptian goddess of mining, was established during the reign of Seti I, second king of the Nineteenth Dynasty, and served the members of the Egyptian mining expeditions and the local workers.

In the temple, archaeologists found hieroglyphic inscriptions, including cartouches of the Egyptian pharaohs who reigned in the second half of the fourteenth through the twelfth centuries BCE. However, with the decline of Egyptian control of the region in the middle of the twelfth century BCE—the time of the invasion of the Sea Peoples and the arrival of the Philistines in Canaan—the mines at Timna and the Hathor temple were abandoned.

They also found a low mound, 15 × 15 meters and about 1.5 meters high, leaning against one of the large, picturesque, Nubian sandstone formations that comprise King Solomon's Pillars, located right in the center of the ancient smelting area of Timna and a popular tourist attraction. The excavation of the small mound was originally planned as a trial and scheduled to take about two weeks. But right from the first day numerous unusual and unexpected finds came to light, causing a complete change of the expedition's plans. The result was a season of more than two months—and the discovery of a temple containing almost ten thousand small finds.

The life story of the temple falls into four main phases: at the beginning, there were several shallow pits and a few fireplaces cut into the bed-rock under the rock shelter formed by the huge over-hanging walls of "King Solomon's Pillars." Flint tools and pottery date this phase to the Chalcolithic period. . . .

More than 2000 years later, . . . an Egyptian temple was erected on top of the Chalcolithic remains. . . . Many architectural frag-ments of this initial phase of the temple survived, some bearing hieroglyphic inscriptions of a Hathor face, the Egyptian goddess to whom the Timna temple was dedicated.

After a thorough wanton destruction, . . . a new temple was built on top of the ruins. . . . There is some evidence that this happened during the reign of Ramses III (1198–1166 BCE). . . .

The second temple, still in use under Ramses V (1160–1156 BCE), was destroyed by an earthquake. After a short period of abandon-ment, the temple worship was renewed [after the temple was cov-ered by a large tent]. . . . There are convincing reasons to relate this tent-sanctuary to the Midianites who returned to Timna for a short while after the Egyptian copper mining expedition no longer reached the area. . . .

This find is of considerable significance for the archaeology and history of the Holy Land and the Bible; it solves a number of long outstanding problems but, in turn, it raises many new questions. We know today that the copper mines of Timna were operated by pharaonic expeditions of the 19th to 20th Dynasties, in collabora-tion with local Kenite-Midianite tribes, and there is no evidence for the existence of any "King Solomon's Mines."[3]

Located in the Timna Valley, twenty miles north of the Gulf of Aqaba on the Red Sea, in an area called Arabah, Solomon's Pillars are natural geographical formations named after the biblical king. As Timna was believed to be the site of copper mining under

King Solomon, the local pillars took this name from him. However, instead of the presumed biblical ties, Solomon's Pillars proved to be related to the pharaohs of Egypt. An inscription near the temple depicts pharaoh Ramses III offering gifts to the goddess Hathor.

As a result of Rothenberg's pioneering work, a new paradigm emerged, one in which the New Kingdom Egyptians, and not King Solomon of Israel, were the true masters of the local copper mines. Nonetheless, this did not stop those who regard the biblical account as more historically accurate from trying to reverse the conclusion again. A report under the title "King Solomon's Mines Rediscovered?" was published by *National Geographic* in October 2008, and it claims that the Timna mines belong to Solomon after all:

> Copper mines in southern Jordan were active centuries earlier than previously believed, according to a new study that suggests the area was producing the metal at the same time as the biblical figure of King Solomon is said to have built Jerusalem's first Jewish temple.
>
> Industrial-scale metal production was occurring at a site in Jordan in the tenth century B.C., according to the study's carbon dating of ancient industrial mining debris and analysis of the settlement layout.
>
> Previous studies had concluded no copper production occurred in the area before the seventh century B.C.
>
> "We're conclusively showing that the Iron Age chronology [of this region] has to be pushed back another 300 years," said lead author Thomas Levy, an anthropologist at the University of California, San Diego.
>
> The shift in estimated Iron Age dates means the Jordan copper mine would have been in operation during the reigns of Kings David and Solomon—who are referred to in the Old Testament (the Hebrew Bible) but have not been verified as actual historical figures.

"Now we have to readdress many of the questions about the relationship between the biblical text about this region in those centuries and the archaeological record," Levy said.[4]

It is significant that a nonbiblical, nonhistorical story is proved to be right by archaeological finds. It is even more significant that Solomon's mines point not to the kings of Israel, but to the pharaohs of Egypt. This shows that Solomon's biblical account, although placed at a different geographical location and a different time, comes from the story of Amenhotep III.

15

Wisdom and Magic

WHILE KING DAVID WAS KNOWN to be a warrior hero, King Solomon became known as a wise man. The Bible says:

> The LORD appeared to Solomon during the night in a dream, and God said, "Ask for whatever you want me to give you." Solomon answered, 'You have shown great kindness to your servant, my father David. . . . You have continued this great kindness to him and have given him a son to sit on his throne this very day. . . . But I am only a little child and do not know how to carry out my duties. . . . So give your servant a discerning heart to govern your people and to distinguish between right and wrong." . . . The LORD was pleased that Solomon had asked for this. So God said to him, "Since you have asked for this and not for life or wealth for yourself, nor have asked for death of your enemies, . . . I will do what you have asked. I will give you a wise and discerning heart, so that there will be never anyone like you, nor will there ever be." (1 Kings 3:5–7, 9–12)

Wisdom is the ability to use one's knowledge and experience to make good decisions and judgments. Later on, a new understanding of Solomon's wisdom appeared in some apocryphal works of unknown authorship. One of these, the Wisdom of Solomon, was even believed to have been written by Solomon himself. However, the Wisdom of Solomon was not written in Solomon's alleged capital, Jerusalem, but in Alexandria in Egypt. Moreover, it is generally dated to the late first century BCE, and it was written not in Hebrew or Aramaic but in Greek, the literary language of Alexandria at the time. Although the Wisdom of Solomon is not part of the Hebrew Bible, it, along with some other works of what is called *wisdom literature,* were incorporated into the Septuagint, the Greek translation of the Old Testament, composed in Alexandria in the third century BCE. Although the Wisdom of Solomon starts with a message addressed to the "rulers of the world" (Wisdom of Solomon 1:1 NRSV), it seems that the actual audience was members of the author's own community.

The book falls into three parts:

1. Superiority of the pious over the godless
2. Identification of Wisdom as a woman
3. The marvels of wisdom

The book opens with the opposed pairs of righteousness/ unrighteousness and death/immortality, warning that those who do not follow righteousness will "reason unsoundly" (Wisdom 2:1 NRSV) and will not be open to wisdom. It states that wisdom is not an inherent human quality, nor is it one that can be taught; it comes from outside, and only to those who are prepared to receive it through righteousness. It also confirms that although the righteous will suffer, they will be rewarded with immortality, while the wicked will die miserably. The unrighteous are doomed because they do not know God's purpose, but the righteous will judge the unrighteous in God's presence.

Here we find a new element: a belief in immortality that is not found in the Torah, the first five books of Moses in the Old Testament. While the Talmud does not consider him to be a prophet, until this day Daniel is not included in the Old Testament scriptures for the Jews. But some five centuries before the supposed date of the birth of Christ, the prophet Daniel, from the captivity of Babylon, uttered a remarkable prophecy: "Multitudes who sleep in the dust of the earth will awake: some to everlasting life, others to shame and everlasting contempt" (Daniel 12:2).

In the Old Testament, man was not originally created mortal, but the divine decree to Adam—stating that he is dust and will return to dust (Genesis 3:19)—implies that physical dissolution is punishment for his disobedience. When Adam sinned by eating from the forbidden tree, he was expelled from the Garden of Eden and denied access to the Tree of Life.

The idea of eternal spiritual life redeemed through faith, however, came only with the New Testament and the belief in Jesus's resurrection: "Whoever lives and believes in me [Christ] will never die" (John 11:26); "Our Savior Christ Jesus . . . destroyed death and brought life and immortality to light through the gospel" (2 Timothy 1:10).

In its second part, the Wisdom of Solomon talks about Wisdom, which is personified as a woman. She is said to have existed "from the beginning of the creation" (Wisdom 6:22 NRSV), and God is her source. She is to be loved and desired. Kings seek her, and Solomon says, "I preferred her to scepters and thrones," and "I loved her more than health and beauty" (Wisdom 7:8, 10 NRSV). In turn, she has always come to the aid of the righteous, from Adam to the Exodus.

Woman as Wisdom in Gnostic and Hermetic philosophy is different than Wisdom personified in the Book of Proverbs. While Proverbs presents Wisdom as fear of God and points us in the direction of scripture, in Gnostic literature it is Wisdom (Sophia) who emanated from eternal light and who is the one who created the God of the Old Testament, creator of the physical world.

The Wisdom of Solomon's characterization of Wisdom as a woman contrasts with the picture of woman given in Genesis, where

Eve disobeys God's command not only by eating from the forbidden tree, but also by persuading Adam to eat from it as well. As a result, both Adam and Eve are expelled from the Garden of Eden and become mortal.

Wisdom became a central theme in philosophy and religion in Alexandria during the early years of the Christian era. In Greek, *Sophia,* "wisdom," is in the feminine gender case. Among the early Gnostic Christian theologies, Sophia is analogous to the human soul but is also one of the feminine aspects of God.

In 1945, an ancient Coptic library was found near the Upper Egyptian town of Nag Hammadi. This library proved to contain some Gnostic writings, including some Christian Gospels that had not been known before. It seems that before the end of the fourth century CE, some Egyptian Christians who were condemned as heretics by orthodox Christianity decided to bury their books, fearing that the authorities would burn unorthodox writings. In the Nag Hammadi texts, Sophia is the lowest Aeon, or anthropic expression of the light of God. She is believed to have fallen from grace in some way, in so doing creating, or helping to create, the material world.

The third and final part of the Wisdom of Solomon deals with the rescue of the righteous, focusing on the Exodus from Egypt: "You [God] have not neglected to help [your people] at all times and in all places" (Wisdom 19:22 NRSV).

SOLOMON'S MAGIC

Along with this new understanding of Solomon's wisdom, another belief arose that regarded Solomon as being an exorcist who practiced magic.

The word *magic* is used seven times in the New International Version of the Bible, three times in the Old Testament and four times in the New Testament; the word *magician* is used twice. Magic—the attempt to exploit supernatural powers by formulaic recitations to achieve goals that are otherwise unrealizable—was seen in a negative light in the Old Testament and was banned under penalty of death (Exodus 22:18). It was held that the deception of magic made the Egyptians believe in the power of their gods. While Genesis speaks of magicians in the pharaoh's service (Genesis 41:8), Exodus speaks of magicians practicing what is called "secret arts" (Exodus 8:7). "So Moses and Aaron went to Pharaoh and did just as the LORD commanded. Aaron threw his staff down in front of Pharaoh and his officials, and it became a snake. Pharaoh then summoned wise men and sorcerers, and the Egyptian magicians also did the same things by their secret arts: Each one threw down his staff and it became a snake. But Aaron's staff swallowed up their staffs" (Exodus 7:10–12).

In the first century CE, texts appeared claiming that Solomon was an exorcist who practiced magic and received the knowledge of how to expel and control demons from God. Nonetheless, these claims have nothing to do with the biblical story of Solomon and were not known before the first century:

> The outsider evidence about Solomon and magical traditions makes evident two details: on the one hand, the exorcistic and demonology content of these traditions constitute the first stage of the link between Solomon and magic, on the other, they provide the terminus *a quo* for establishing such a link in literary works. These texts can be dated around the first century C.E. . . . The dating of the *Wisdom of Solomon* around the second quarter of the first century C.E. reinforces *the terminus a quo* of these traditions about Solomon as exorcist.
>
> However, the main source for these traditions is Josephus's narrative of exorcism performed by an Essene in front of Vespasian in Book 8 of his *Jewish Antiquities*. This text shows several traits about Solomon and his esoteric knowledge that will keep appearing in

other texts. Josephus [a Jewish historian who lived in the first century CE] mentions that God gave Solomon knowledge of exorcism:

"And God granted him knowledge of the art used against the demons for the benefit and healing of men. He also composed incantations by which illnesses are relieved, and left behind forms of exorcism with which those possessed by demons drive them out, never to return. And this kind of cure is of very great power among us to this day" (AJ [Antiquities Josephus] 8.45–46).

Josephus's position towards magic and esoteric arts is generally negative. However, here he gives a characterization of Solomon that shows him to be linked with exorcism and magical healing. The exact wording of the text is revealing; Josephus's use of the present tense in the narrative marks it as actual and referring to the time of the author. . . . Somehow Josephus "felt" compelled to include such a practice, despite his overall negative opinion about those operations.[1]

One object believed to have been used by the king to give him special power was his royal seal. This ring gave Solomon the power to command demons and spirits and to speak with animals. It was often depicted in the shape of a pentagram or a hexagram, the latter in the form of the Star of David (also known as the Seal of Solomon). Because of the proverbial wisdom of Solomon, the design of this signet ring came to be seen as an amulet or talisman in medieval and Renaissance magic, occultism, and alchemy. The Star of David as a symbol of Judaism in modern times has its origins in fourteenth-century depictions of the Seal of Solomon.

The date and origin of the Seal of Solomon are not known, although a legend of a magic ring with which the possessor could command demons was known in the first century CE. But this was not associated with Solomon before medieval times, when Arab writers related that the ring was given to the king from heaven. This ring was made from brass and iron, and the two parts were used to seal written commands to good and evil spirits, respectively.

The Qur'an, which appeared in the seventh century CE, states that Solomon had under his rule not only humans but also hosts of jinn (spirits): "And for Solomon the wind blows with his command . . . and of the demons, those who dive for him and do more things, and we [God] protect them" (21:81–82). According to the Qur'an, Solomon was also able to understand the language of the birds and ants and to see some of the hidden glory in the world that was not accessible to ordinary human beings.

EGYPTIAN WISDOM AND MAGIC

Egypt's reputation as a repository of wisdom is ancient. In the frame narrative of Plato's *Timaeus,* we read that because of its great antiquity, Egypt preserves historical knowledge that has elsewhere been lost. Its outstanding governance, moreover, is the closest real approximation to Plato's ideal state, for, here, life is regulated by law according to the model of the macrocosm. In other cultures knowledge has been periodically obliterated by natural catastrophes, while the Egyptians retain access to antediluvian knowledge. . . . According to the story, the first Hermes wrote down the ancient knowledge in hieroglyphs before the Flood. . . .[2]

Already in late antiquity Hermes Trismegistus had made a name for himself as a magician, and Arabic magical texts often claimed to be Hermetic writings. In the frame narrative of the *Picatrix,* we read that the ancient Egyptian-Hermetic wisdom was so powerful a magical instrument that it had to be encoded by writing it down in hieroglyphs. Hermes' magical abilities are illustrated in a tale of the Copts, who were themselves reputed to be experts in science. They knew five persons named Hermes, who were responsible for many legendary cultural innovations.[3]

Most of what we know about Solomon's magic in antiquity comes from Gnostic and Hermetic sources. The *Testament of Truth,* one of the Nag Hammadi texts, says that Solomon commanded demons to build Jerusalem:

> They are wicked in their behaviour! Some of them fall away [to the worship of] idols. [Others] have [demons] dwelling with them, [as did] David the king. He is the one who laid the foundation of Jerusalem; and his son Solomon, *whom he begat in [adultery],* is one who built Jerusalem by means of demons, because he received [power]. When he [had finished building, he imprisoned] the demons [in the temple]. He [placed them] into seven [waterpots]. [They remained] a long [time in] the [waterpots], abandoned [there]. When the Romans [went] up to [Jerusalem], they discovered [the] waterpots, [and immediately] the [demons] ran out of the waterpots, as those who escape from prison. . . . [And] since those days [they dwell] with men who are [in] ignorance, and [they have remained upon] the earth.
>
> Who, then, is [David]? And who is Solomon? [And] what is the foundation? And what is the wall which surrounds Jerusalem? And who are the demons? And what are the waterpots? And who are the Romans? But these [are mysteries].[4]

It seems that these early Egyptian Christians took the names of David and Solomon as symbols, hiding their real historical identity. Note also that contrary to the biblical account, which reports the death of David's and Bathsheba's infant son, conceived in adultery, this text claims that the Solomon himself was that child.

During the early Christian era, Christian followers of the Hermetic traditions also practiced magic (which was considered to be an aspect of pagan wisdom) and regarded magicians as wise men.

Arabic texts present Hermes as a magician and conjurer, and sometimes as a god.⁵ An example of the latter is *The Great Circular Letter of the Spheres of Hermes of Dendera*. At the beginning of the text Hermes says: "I am the master of Wonders, who built the seven spheres on top of one another, who seized the beaming sun and the sinning moon and planted the tree of light-filled wisdom. He who eats of its fruits will not go hungry but can do without food and drink, he will be spiritual and divine; his knowledge will never be exhausted, and his good deeds will never cease."⁶

From the above information, it is clear that the nonbiblical accounts of Solomon's wisdom and magic appeared in Egypt during the early part of the Christian era. Wisdom and magic played a major part in ancient Egypt, as well as in the early years of its adoption of Christianity. The ancient Egyptian word *heka,* "magic," is the source of the modern Arabic word *hekma,* meaning "wisdom." This was believed to be one of the forces used by the creator to make the world. Priests were the main practitioners of magic in pharaonic Egypt, where they were seen as the guardians of the secret knowledge given by the gods to humanity to ward off the blows of fate. They were seen to be in possession of secret knowledge that had been given to them by the gods.

Authors Manfred Horstmanshoff and Marten Stol discuss magic in a medical context:

Magic and religion, which were virtually indistinguishable contents in ancient Egypt, played a significant role in medical practice. . . . As early as the third century BCE, some Greek writers tried to distinguish between "rational" medicine and "irrational" treatment based on superstition of divine intervention. However, the Egyptians would have regarded this as a meaningless distinction; generally, they treated diseases according to the perceived cause, and thus pragmatic means were adopted for conditions where the reason was evident (such as the use of bone setting and simple surgery for trauma), whereas magic was employed to alleviate afflictions such as headaches where the cause was obscure and might be attributable to a supernatural agent. . . .

According to one definition, magic is "the power of apparently using supernatural forces to change the form of things or influence events." The Egyptians believed that the divine creative word and magical energy could be used to turn concepts into reality.[7]

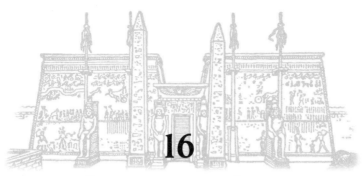

16

The Lost Palace

WE HAVE HISTORICAL AND ARCHAEOLOGICAL EVIDENCE of building during the reign of Amenhotep III that matches the building attributed to Solomon and shows that biblical scholars, historians, and archaeologists have been confused by the biblical account and have been seeking evidence of David and Solomon in the wrong century.

According to the biblical story, King Solomon's prosperity and success were achieved through financial windfalls from taxation, tribute, and gifts from foreign countries under his influence. Thus Solomon was able to accumulate fourteen hundred chariots and twelve thousand horses, which he kept in the chariot cities of the empire as well as in Jerusalem. The king also made silver and gold "as common in Jerusalem as stones," and made cedar as abundant as the sycamores, which are in the lowland (2 Chronicles 1:15).

Having inherited a great empire with no wars to fight, King Solomon is said to have used his great wealth to establish many buildings throughout the empire as well as in Jerusalem. Solomon also had hundreds of women in his harem, including foreign princesses he married to cement alliances with foreign rulers of his empire. And, although Jerusalem in his time was a small fortress perched on top of a ridge, just south of a flat rocky surface, Solomon managed to build his great royal palace, as well as his Temple, on the enclosed area to its north—the Temple Mount.

The building of Solomon's palace took thirteen years to finish, twice as long as it took to build the Temple, and was much more complicated. It was not just a residence for the king, but a whole complex of buildings, with many different functions.

According to the Bible, this royal palace was so magnificent that "when the queen of Sheba had seen . . . the house that he [Solomon] had built, the food on his table, the seating of his officials, and the attending servants in their robes, the cupbearers in their robes, and the burnt offerings he made at the temple of the LORD, she was overwhelmed" (2 Chronicles 9:3–4).

PALACE SIMILARITIES

From the account in 1 Kings 7:2–12 we can see that Solomon's palace consisted of five elements: (1) the king's palace; (2) the house of the pharaoh's daughter, "whom he had married"; (3) the throne room; (4) a hall of columns; and (5) the house of the forest of Lebanon. The foundations were of costly stones, while pillars of Lebanon cedar supported the roofs.

Up to the time of Amenhotep III, although Thebes was the religious and administrative capital of Egypt, the main royal residence was at Memphis, on the western branch of the Nile, a few miles to the south of the Great Pyramid of Giza. With the vast wealth of his empire at his disposal and no wars to fight, Amenhotep III embarked on the construction of a great royal complex in western Thebes. His own palace was ready by year 8 (1398 BCE) of his reign, but the whole complex was not completed until his year 30 (in 1375 BCE). The area of the palace was excavated between 1910 and 1920 by the Egyptian Expedition of the Metropolitan Museum of Art of New York. From these excavations we can see that, although they form part of a much larger complex, the five elements ascribed to Solomon's palace are to be found in Amenhotep III's palace at Thebes.

The King's Palace

This was the oldest and most important building, occupying the southeast quarter and adjoined on the east by its kitchens, offices, and storerooms. It had also a section for the king's harem and was connected with a smaller palace, the residence of Queen Tiye, daughter of the king's high official, Yuya.

The House of the Pharaoh's Daughter

As we saw before, Amenhotep III married his sister Sitamun, the daughter of Tuthmosis IV, in order to gain his right to the throne, which was the Egyptian custom. The American scholar William C. Hayes commented in an article in the *Journal of Near Eastern Studies* in 1951: "The great North Palace . . . appears to have been the residence of an extremely important royal lady, quite possibly Queen Sitamun."[1]

The Throne Room

The reception quarters consist of a large, squarish hall with many rows of columns in wood; a throne dais set along the axis of the entrance corridor; a second, smaller hypostyle (columned) hall with a throne dais near it; a throne room; and a bedroom.

The Hall of Pillars

Hayes describes this as "the royal Audience Pavilion, its floor elevated above the surrounding terrain, its northern façade provided with a balcony-like projection jutting out into a deep, colonnaded courtyard."

The Palace of the Forest of Lebanon

This was, according to Hayes, a "Festival hall, prepared for the celebration of Amenhotep III's second *sed* [rejuvenation] festival," a big colonnaded building that extended from the very north of the palace complex. The complex also included houses for other members of the royal family as well as for court officials and servants. Exactly as the Bible says, all the pillars were of cedar wood imported from Lebanon. Alexander Badawy, an Egyptian scholar, gives a detailed description of the hall in his book *A History of Egyptian Architecture:* "Ceilings were of timber rafters, covered beneath with lath and plaster and painted with a series of protecting Nekhebet vultures in the official halls and in the bedroom of Pharaoh, or with vines within a frame of rosettes and chequered pattern, spirals and bulls' heads, similar to Aegean ornament. Floors were decorated in the same technique to represent a pool, papyrus, lotus and fowl."[2]

ARCHAEOLOGICAL EVIDENCE?

In 2010, it was believed that remains of Solomon's palace were found in Jerusalem:

> A 3,000-year-old defensive wall possibly built by King Solomon has been unearthed in Jerusalem, according to the Israeli archaeologist who led the excavation. . . .
>
> The tenth-century BCE wall is 230 feet (70 meters) long and about 6 meters (20 feet) tall. It stands along what was then the edge of Jerusalem—between the Temple Mount, still Jerusalem's paramount landmark, and the ancient City of David, today a modern-day Arab neighborhood called Silwan. . . .
>
> The new discovery is the first archaeological evidence for this structure, Mazar says.
>
> Ancient artifacts found in and around the complex pointed Mazar to the tenth-century BCE date: "We don't have many kings during the tenth century that could have built such a structure, basically just David and Solomon," she said.[3]

Nevertheless, as Mazar found no indications of Solomon in the site, the mere existence of the wall did not convince other archaeologists of her claim.

Half a century prior, the British archaeologist Kathleen Kenyon succeeded in uncovering the remains of the Millo (2 Samuel 5:9). These were supporting terraces inserted to widen the upper surface of the rock on which the ancient fortress of Jerusalem was built by extending its limits toward the sloping ground to the east. Kenyon was also able to date the first construction of the Millo to the fourteenth century BCE—the time of Amenhotep III.

A few years later, when no other remains of Solomon's palace were found in Jerusalem, some archaeologists tried to see if they could find it anywhere else in Israel. On September 1, 2016, Israel's Haaretz news service reported the possible discovery of Solomon's palace, not in Jerusalem, but in Gezer, between Jerusalem and Tel Aviv. The report says that a monumental palace was found dated to three thousand years ago, from the tenth century BCE. "A team of United States archaeologists have been working on the structure, positioned to the west of the city's so-called Solomonic Gate, for several years. They now uncovered the remains of a building consisting of a series of spacious rooms arranged around two long central courtyards."[4] The archaeologists are trying to find some elements to connect King Solomon with this building.

If Solomon built his temple in his capital Jerusalem, why are these archaeologists trying to find his palace in Gezer? And where should they be looking instead?

SOLOMON'S EGYPTIAN PALACE

Although modern archaeologists have failed to find any remains of Solomon's house in Jerusalem, physical remains of this palace, as described in the Bible, were discovered in Upper Egypt.

As I have argued before, *Solomon* was not the original name of the king mentioned in the Bible. He was only called by this name, which means "king of peace," later, as his reign over the great empire stretching between the upper Euphrates, in northern Syria, and Egypt was a peaceful time for all the area. If we look at the times and character of Pharaoh Amenhotep III, we find evidence confirming the biblical account not in Jerusalem but in Thebes, four centuries earlier.

Almost all of what we know about King Solomon from the biblical account is historically confirmed in the life of Amenhotep III. Both kings inherited a large empire between northern Syria and Egypt and no longer had to fight to keep it. Both men had hundreds of women in their harem, with some princesses as wives, including a daughter of the pharaoh. Both kings engaged in major building projects, including a great royal palace and a major temple. The only difference is that while the Bible places the king's reign in Canaan during the tenth century BCE, evidence for this individual is found in Egypt during the fourteenth century BCE.

Amenhotep III, like Solomon, established a great royal house and a large temple in the same location, at Medinet Habu, in western Thebes (modern Luxor). Amenhotep III moved residence from Memphis to Thebes, and this is where he built his own palace, "The Radiance of Aten," later to become "The House of Rejoicing." This palace is known today as Malqata. Built on thirty-two hectares, it comprises four separate palaces that served different purposes: one for the harem; one for the officials and administration of his court; one for the pharaoh's personal apartments; and one for the quarters of the slaves and stewards and for a temple of Amun. According to the archaeological report made by the northern California chapter of the American Research Center in Egypt: "The reign of Amenhotep III saw several major innovations in how the pharaoh chose to represent himself. Amenhotep III closely identified himself with Re, the sun god. He was a prolific builder of temples in both Egypt and Nubia and the statuary that decorated them. . . . The immense images guarding the entrance, the so-called 'Colossi of Memnon' give silent testimony to the temple's original size. Amenhotep III popularized statuary that combined human bodies with the heads of animals to represent gods. He was the first Pharaoh to become defied."[5]

The modern name given to the site of the ancient Egyptian palace complex of Amenhotep III is Malqata, whose name means "place of meeting." It is located on the west bank of the Nile at Thebes in Upper Egypt, in the desert to the south of Medinet Habu. Construction of the palace began around year 11 of the king's reign, while he was living at Memphis, and continued until he moved there permanently around his year 29.

The palace complex contained many audience halls, central halls, courtyards, villas, smaller palace complexes for the royal family, and apartments for officials. The royal apartment featured a bedroom, a dressing room, a private audience chamber, and a harem. The palace had a central courtyard, and across from the pharaoh's rooms were apartments for his daughters and son. His Great Royal Wife, Tiye, had her own smaller palace complex diagonally across from the pharaoh's. The palace grounds contained gardens and a large pleasure lake.

Malqata was managed by a veritable army of servants and staff. Remains of kitchens near the royal chamber have been found, as well as servants' quarters. The palace resembled a complete city, with officials in charge of different sections, such as the gardens and the different apartments and quarters.

The site of Malqata is certainly on scale with other of Amenhotep III's ambitious projects. Seven kilometers in length, Malqata was a palace-city that included a temple, houses for the elite, several palaces, villages, several ceremonial structures, a royal road, a causeway, and the immense harbor known as Birket Habu. Malqata was expressly built for the celebration of the pharaoh's *heb-sed,* or jubilee, a festival during the thirtieth year of his reign.

Malqata was not located on virgin soil: it seems that Amenhotep III dismantled existing shrines and structures to build his palace-city. This suggests that the area already was significant to the Egyptians, which may have been one of the reasons why it was chosen.

The king's palace must have been a stunning and impressive building, colorfully decorated with painted plaster ceilings and walls. Many scenes incorporated design elements borrowed from outside Egypt, including the Aegean islands. The Egypt of Amenhotep III was a very cosmopolitan society, having a thriving trade with Crete, Syro-Palestine, and Africa, and acquiring materials that traveled as far as three thousand miles from Afghanistan, which was the source of the much-prized stone lapis lazuli. Part of the king's palace at Malqata was a two-storied structure; this is indicated by the remains of two different ceiling paintings lying one over the other. The palace's central hall had two rows of columns and a dais at one end. Beyond that was a set of rooms believed to belong to the king. The king's bedroom had a floor paved with stone slabs and decorated walls that were preserved to a significant height in 1910, though they are now lost. Tree pits indicating gardens were discovered behind these rooms at the south side of the palace.

Other structures in the Malqata complex include the North Palace, sometimes called the Queen's Palace, a raised mound referred to as an audience pavilion, and the North and South Villages. The North Village was an unplanned settlement, possibly housing workers for manufacture and food production and to support other court activities. The South Village was the name given to a huge mound of debris, which is now gone, as it was used for *sebbakh* (decayed mud brick, employed by villagers as fertilizer). It was most likely also a center for craftsmen.

When we compare the Malqata, the great palace built by

Amenhotep III at Western Thebes, with the biblical description of Solomon's royal palace in Jerusalem, it becomes clear that Malqata was the royal residence described by the biblical narrator. Along with his Malqata palace, and adjacent to it, Amenhotep III, like King Solomon, built his great temple.

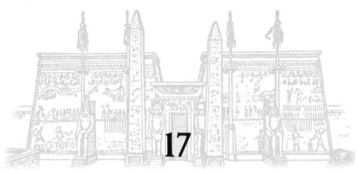

17

The Temples
of Solomon and
Amenhotep III

ACCORDING TO THE BIBLE, Solomon carried out some major buildings operations in Jerusalem, including his Temple; his own royal residence; a palace for his queen, the pharaoh's daughter; a throne room (1 Kings 7:7); a portico, or porch of pillars (1 Kings 7:6); and the "Palace of the Forest of Lebanon" (1 Kings 7:2). These were all built at the same time, in one location.

Solomon's Temple, the Bible says, was established as the center of worship for Yahweh in all Israel: its Holy of Holies was the place where he situated the Ark of the Covenant, including the original tablets of the Ten Commandments. Different books of the Old Testament describe the Temple, how it was built, and how it gradually became the central location of worship for the twelve tribes of Israel during the United Monarchy.

Solomon is said to have begun to build the Temple in the fourth year of his reign, while its construction took seven years. Although different sources give different accounts regarding the size of each part of the Temple, its main features are agreed upon.

THE LAYOUT OF
SOLOMON'S TEMPLE

According to *Easton's Bible Dictionary* and the *Jewish Encyclopaedia,* the Temple was composed of:

1. The *debir.* Called the "inner house" or the "Holy of Holies," it was considered the dwelling place of the name of God. It was floored and wainscoted with cedar wood from Lebanon, and its floor and windows were overlaid with gold. It contained two cherubim, each having outspread wings so that they stood side by side and their wings touched the wall on either side and met in the center of the room. The Ark of the Covenant, containing the original tablets of the Ten Commandments, was placed in the Holy of Holies.
2. The *hekal.* The holy place, called the "greater house" or the "temple." Its walls were lined with cedar, on which were carved figures of cherubim, palm trees, and open flowers, which were also overlaid with gold.
3. The *ulam.* The porch, or entrance, before the Temple on the east, where the two pillars stood.
4. The chambers. Built around the Temple on the southern, western, and northern sides, these rooms were used for storage.

Biblical tradition says that the building was surrounded by the "court of the priests," called the "inner court," and the "great court," which in turn surrounded the whole temple. It is stated that the Temple was provided with a structure around it. In addition, in front of the Temple, a little to the southeast, stood the "sea," a large laver of cast metal ornamented with gourds (1 Kings 7:24). This laver, which rested on the back of twelve bulls, had a capacity of three thousand *baths* (a Hebrew measure of volume) for the ablutions of the priests.

Two Pillars

Moreover, Solomon's Temple had some special features, the nature of which became subject to much argument and speculation. It is stated that in the porch, before the Temple, Solomon erected two pillars named Jachin and Boaz (1 Kings 7:21). These two pillars became the most widely discussed feature of Solomon's Temple, as they must have had a hidden symbolic function. Why were the pillars given names at all, and what do these names mean?

Different scholars have had different views about the possible meaning of the names given to these two pillars. Some explained these names by saying that it was the custom among ancient Middle Eastern peoples to give names to sacred objects. Josephus, in *Antiquities of the Jews,* says the name of Boaz, which stood on the left when one was facing the Temple, means "in strength," and that of Jachin, which stood on the right, means "will establish."

Cherubim

At the same time, although it was forbidden for the Israelites to make images, the Temple of Solomon is said to have included cherubim everywhere, even in the Holy of Holies. Pertaining to the arrangement of the cherubim in the debir, 2 Chronicles 3:13 says that "they faced the main hall." The cherubim, who are not given angelic status in the Old Testament, were regarded as unearthly beings who directly attend to God. Although the word *cherubim* appears ninety-one times in the Hebrew Bible, the Scriptures do not describe them, and their role is never explicitly elucidated. While still in Egypt, Yahweh tells Moses to make multiple images of cherubim at specific points around the Ark of the Covenant (Exodus 25:18–22). The cherubim were two figures placed on top of the Ark, which had been set in the holiest place in the tabernacle, established by Moses at the foot of Mount Sinai. Exodus 25:20 states that the two figures had "their faces turned to each other."

Masonic Details

Other details of the Temple are not found in the Bible. As Solomon's Temple represents one of the focus points in modern Freemasonry, the Masons had their own understanding of its construction:

> King David began the temple. . . . Upon the accession of Solomon to the Israelitish throne, he pushed forward with vigour the projects of his father, and hastened the completion of the temple. This king collected from various countries of the world a larger class of skilled workmen, who numbered fourscore thousand hewers of stone. Among other charges made by Solomon, he selected three thousand of the most expert operatives, and placed them as governors or superintendents of the work. All these were classed under the general term of Masons. At this time, Solomon received many flattering indications of the friendly spirit of neighboring rulers, and among others, Hiram, King of Tyre, who offered him the resources of the Tyrian kingdom. By this means the king of Israel was enabled to procure such timber as was essential in the construction of the temple. A son of Hiram, Anynon, by name, was appointed master mason of this great work, and was especially distinguished for his geometric knowledge. He was chief master of all the masons engaged in the erection of the Jewish temple, and was a proficient master of engraving and carving, and all manner of masonry required for the sacred edifice. . . . In this manner, the worthy science of masonry was introduced into the country of Jerusalem, and then propagated throughout many kingdoms.[1]

DESTRUCTION

A few years following the death of King Solomon, the Bible says that what became known as the United Kingdom came to an end on the succession of Solomon's son Rehoboam, around 930 BCE. Simultaneously, Solomon's great empire vanished in a moment as if it had never existed.

The Israelites then were divided in two separate kingdoms; the kingdom of Israel (ruled by Jeroboam) in the north, including Shechem and Samaria, and the kingdom of Judah in the south (ruled by Rehoboam), including Jerusalem. As a result, Solomon's Temple was no longer the center of Israelite worship, as King Jeroboam of Israel built different shrines on different high places (1 Kings 12:26–28, 31).

Although it is known that the Egyptians built temples since the beginning of their history, Solomon's Temple was a new thing in Israelite history, because previously the Israelites had always worshipped on high places. The earliest biblical mention of a site of worship is found in Genesis 12:6–8, where Abraham builds altars in the places where the Lord appears to him. As we have seen, Abraham was also ordered by the Lord to sacrifice Sarah's son on a high mountain (Genesis 22:2). According to Genesis 28:18–19, Jacob set up a pillar to the Lord at Bethel and poured oil on its top, and the prophet Samuel "went on a circuit from Bethel to Gilgal to Mizpah, judging Israel in all these places" (1 Samuel 7:16).

Solomon himself worshipped on different high places: "As Solomon grew old, his wives turned his heart after other gods, and his heart was not fully devoted to the LORD his God. . . . So Solomon did evil in the eyes of the LORD. . . . On a hill east of Jerusalem, Solomon built a high place for Chemosh the detestable god of Moab, and for Molek the detestable god of the Ammonites. He did the same for all his foreign wives, who burned incense and offered sacrifices to their gods" (1 Kings 11:4–8).

Moreover, following Solomon's death, the Israelites went back to worship on the same high places where they used to worship before. Jeroboam, king of Israel in the north, "made two golden calves. He said to the people, 'It is too much for you to go up to Jerusalem. Here are your gods, Israel, who brought you up out of Egypt.' One he set up in Bethel, and the other in Dan. . . . The people came to worship the one in Bethel and went as far as Dan to worship the other. . . . Jeroboam built shrines on high places and appointed priests from all sorts of people, even though they were not Levites" (1 Kings 12:28–31).

Nothing much is known about the fate of Solomon's Temple after the king's death aside from the biblical accounts that indicate that the Israelites moved their worship to different high places. In the meantime, it is generally believed that the Temple survived until the time of the Babylonian invasion in 586 BCE. Following the Babylonian Exile, when Cyrus the Great of Persia defeated the Babylonians, he gave the Jews permission to return to Palestine and build their temple on the site of the earlier Temple, which was completed before the end of the sixth century BCE. The Jerusalem Temple became the center of Jewish worship in Palestine until it was destroyed in 70 CE by the Romans.

In modern times, discrepancies in the biblical account of Solomon's Temple have been questioned by some scholars, who have noticed that "the architectural and ornamental features of the Temple itself, as they make their appearance in Masonic tradition and the biblical account, [were] established . . . with rabbinic legend and exposition, and with present-day biblical commentary and criticism. Here, again, we will note some corroboration, and some discrepancy between several Books of the Bible themselves, and between the various versions and translations; also, some anachronisms and improbabilities."[2] Moreover, modern archaeologists have not been able to find remains of either Solomon's Temple or his palace in Jerusalem.

In his *Archaeology of Palestine,* W. F. Albright—who has been described by another worker in that field as "one of the most competent and versatile archaeologists of the modern world"—tells us that "the age of Solomon was certainly one of the most flourishing periods of material civilization in the history of Palestine."[3] It is not surprising, therefore, that John Garstang has found sufficient material at his command to devote an entire work to the subject.[4] But this appraisal of Albright's is mainly based on the biblical record itself, since contemporaneous extrabiblical chronicles are strangely silent with respect to this period, as J. Mckee Adams has shown.[5] With respect to any extraneous references to David and Solomon in the annals of the neighboring states—and despite the close ties that David, and especially Solomon, are said to have had with Phoenicia and Egypt—it is as if these two Jewish kings had never lived.

One short reference to Sheshonq I, king of Egypt—the "Shishak" of the Bible (1 Kings 14:25–26)—does, however, have some, if limited, significance in this respect. It is Sheshonq, or Shishak, who gave his daughter to Solomon in marriage, making her at the same time a gift of the town of Gezer, which he had conquered and destroyed. Sheshonq is said to have subsequently invaded Palestine after the death of Solomon and sacked the king's palace and the royal buildings, as well as the Temple. Nevertheless, the Great Karnak Relief, on the walls of Luxor, lists the towns Sheshonq conquered in this campaign. It shows the pharaoh before his god Amun, smiting the Asiatics, but the inscription indicates nothing specifically of Solomonic identification, and we are confined entirely to the story in the Bible itself for the other details enumerated. Solomon himself is nowhere mentioned in the record at Karnak.

Similarly, archaeological excavations have so far turned up no unquestionable evidence that the Temple ever existed. The same can be said about Solomon's other building projects in Jerusalem, all of which are said to have "occupied him for a period of twenty years."[6] As Paul Leslie Garber states, "The evidence, such as it is, is of literary character." Albright states pointedly, "No certain traces of the Temple of Solomon . . . have so far been recovered by archaeologists."[7]

EGYPTIAN TEMPLES

The situation in Egypt was different than in Canaan. Egyptians are known to have built temples from the dawn of their history more than five thousand years ago. The ancient Egyptians believed their temples were houses for the gods or kings to whom they were dedicated. The temple was considered the "horizon" of a divine being, the place where the god came into existence at creation.

According to the Bible, much precious material was used in the construction of Solomon's Temple. This is equally true of the mortuary temple that Amenhotep III built in western Thebes. Egyptian temples were built with stone so that they would last forever. The most important part was the sanctuary, which contained a cult image, a statue of the god. The typical design consisted of a series of enclosed halls, open courts, and entrance pylons aligned along the path used for festival processions. Every Egyptian temple followed the same basic design: a forecourt and reception area for public gatherings, with colonnades leading to smaller rooms, which led to the Holy of Holies, where the god was believed to reside when visiting Earth. Within their temples, the Egyptians performed different rituals, gave offerings to the gods, reenacted mythological events through festivals, and performed rites to ward off the forces of chaos. Beyond the temple proper, they used to have an outer wall enclosing a wide variety of secondary buildings. Over time, the Egyptian temple developed, and the rooms outside the sanctuary grew larger. Egyptian temples reached the high point of their design during the time of the New Kingdom and the Eighteenth Dynasty.

Medinet Habu, where Amenhotep III built his house and his mortuary temple, has many features that are identical to those of the descriptions of the Temple of Solomon, including the Migdol Gateway, an exact copy of the Temple of Solomon, and a Holy of Holies, as well as a treasury, and the two pillars (statues) at the eastern gate. The following description shows the Egyptian features of Solomon's Temple.

In the principal front was an ulam [a porch], probably a grand portico, such as they had formerly been in several Egyptian Temples.

The temples of the ancients were generally without windows . . . that of Jerusalem appears to have had them . . . of the same form as those observed in the . . . great temple of Thebes. The timbers of the ceiling were of cedar, and it appears that the roof was flat like Egyptian temples. . . .

Before the ulam were two pillars of brass, whose capitals resembled, according to the expression of the Bible, "lily work," which indicates some resemblance to the Egyptian capitals, composed from lotus flowers. There is no mention of bases, and it is probable that they had none. They were no doubt intended as a decoration to the whole, like the obelisks which were placed before the Egyptian temples.

The exterior walls of the temple were of stone, squared at right angles, and ornamented with the figures of cherubim, palm-leaves . . . sculptured probably in the stone like the Egyptian hieroglyphics.[8]

Although Solomon's Temple had nothing to correspond to an Egyptian hypostyle hall, his palace is said to have had one. The Palace of the Forest of Lebanon and the Hall of Pillars remind one strongly of the outer and inner hypostyle hall of an Egyptian temple. (A hypostyle hall is a space covered by a roof supported by pillars.) Also, the chambers that surrounded the Holy Place in Solomon's Temple, believed to have been storehouses for sacred treasure, are paralleled by similar chambers in Egyptian temples, which surrounded the *naos,* or hypostyle hall, and were used for similar purposes.

AMENHOTEP III'S TEMPLES

On the subject of the riches used by Amenhotep III in his construction of the temples, Donald B. Redford, the Canadian Egyptologist, says in his book *Akhenaten: The Heretic King:* "The recorded figures of metals and precious stones that went into the Montu temple (one of the Karnak temples) is quite staggering: 3.25 tons of electrum, 2.5 tons of gold, 924 tons of copper, 1,250 pounds of lapis lazuli, 215 pounds of turquoise, 1.5 tons of bronze and over 10 tons of beaten copper. Such was the return on Egypt's investment in an empire!"[9]

Amenhotep III, whom I am identifying with the biblical Solomon, is known to have built many temples both in Egypt and in Canaan. He began his building program in his year 2. The sites of his temples for different deities, including himself, were at Hermopolis, opposite Amarna (the new capital that was later founded by his son, Akhenaten), two temples at Karnak to the north of Thebes, the great Luxor temple in Thebes itself, three temples in Nubia, and his mortuary temple north of his palace complex in western Thebes. He also built other, small temples in almost all the Canaanite cities that had Egyptian garrisons, as well as on the Temple Mount in Jerusalem, where his great-grandfather, Tuthmosis III, had kept the Ark of Amun.

Amenhotep III's buildings were of mammoth size and scale and used a copious amount of rich goods as well as the highest quality in design and workmanship. His major achievements in building were the temple at Luxor, his mortuary temple, and the palace at Malqata.

THE LUXOR TEMPLE

The temple complex in ancient Thebes (present-day Luxor), on the western bank of the Nile, is regarded as the greatest of Amenhotep III's building achievements. Started by Amenhotep III, it was completed by Tutankhamun and Ramses II. It was known in the ancient Egyptian language as *ipet resyt*, "the southern sanctuary." The temple also had a Sun Court, which opened to the sky for solar worship. The Luxor complex was not dedicated to a cult god or a deified version of the king in death, but to the rejuvenation of kingship. Here many of the later kings of Egypt were crowned, in reality or conceptually.

(Alexander the Great, who claimed he was crowned at Luxor, may never have visited the temple.)

The Luxor complex was built to mark the celebration of the Opet festival, which brought together the Theban trinity of Amun, Mut, and Khonsu. A cult statue of Amun was paraded down the Nile from the nearby Karnak temple to stay for a while with his consort Mut in a celebration of fertility.

Amenhotep III also used the Luxor temple to show his connection with the gods, as he identified himself with the national deities and indeed presented himself as the substitute for major gods. In a series of scenes, the pharaoh depicts his divine birth, with his mother being offered the ankh, the sign of life. Amenhotep used this as a way not of justifying his rule, but of proclaiming his own status and power as a god.

THE MORTUARY TEMPLE

It is Amenhotep's mortuary temple on the western bank of the Nile, certainly the most impressive of all Egyptian temples, that is to be identified with the biblical Temple. According to the Bible, much precious material was used in the construction of Solomon's temple in Jerusalem. This is equally true of the mortuary temple that Amenhotep III built at western Thebes. Like the latter, the mortuary temple is oriented toward the east and was built on the same location as the royal palace.

Amenhotep III wanted to be revered as a god, not merely in the afterlife, but also on Earth. He built this enormous mortuary temple to leave a legacy that he was a living god who ruled on Earth. Although most of it has disappeared by now, its description gives some clue to its extravagance: "Fine white sandstone, wrought with gold throughout, its floor is adorned with silver, all its portal with electrum . . . it is numerous in royal statues of Elephantine granite of costly gritstone, of every splendid costly stone, established as everlasting works.

Their statue shines more than the heavens; their rays are in the faces [of men]."

The temple was probably the largest ever created in the world and included many different sections. Its storehouse was filled with male and female slaves, and with children of the princesses of all the countries of the captivity of pharaoh. Its storehouses contained cattle as numerous as the sand of the shore.[10] It was surrounded by settlements of Syrians and colonized with children of princes.

The mortuary temple of Amenhotep III is located on the western bank of the Nile, across from the city of Luxor on the eastern bank. In its time, it was the largest funerary complex in Thebes. Currently, only parts of the temple's layout remain, as well as the two Colossi of Memnon, which are two large stone statues placed at the entrance measuring eighteen meters (fifty-nine feet) high. The mortuary temple was built close to the river, and the annual flooding has caused the site to decay at a relatively rapid rate over time.

Throughout the temple, there are hundreds of freestanding statues, sphinxes, and massive stelae. Some of these include numerous statues of Sekhmet, the lion-headed goddess; a lion-crocodile sphinx; jackals; scarab beetles; a white hippopotamus; and other Egyptian gods, along with Amenhotep III himself, represented as a god.

It seems that Amenhotep III organized the animal and Sekhmet statues into maps of the heavens, bringing the heavens to Earth. Jean Yoyotte, the French Egyptologist, suggested that the goddess Sekhmet is given importance not only because she is the "mistress of darkness," but also because she possesses healing qualities, which are meant to cure any illness of the pharaoh's.

It seems that this temple was built to resemble a mound, symbolizing the emergence of the world from the primeval waters of creation. Every time the Nile flooded, the temple emerged from it, as the Egyptians believed that the Earth was formed by a mound emerging from the water.

TWO PILLARS REVISITED

At the front of the temple, the Colossi of Memnon can be found, followed by the long hypostyle hall that leads to the Sun Court. The whole area is surrounded by three pylons, or gates. The Sun Court is divided into northern and southern halves and contained statues of both Amenhotep III and Egyptian gods. The north side had statues made of brown quartzite from Lower Egypt, while the south side had red granite from Aswan in Upper Egypt. Since Amenhotep III revered the sun god, the temple faced the east, and the two colossi in front of it receive the first rays of the rising sun.

The colossi present a difference between Solomon's Temple and the mortuary temple of Amenhotep III. Because the Second Commandment forbade the making of idols, the Bible referred to them as pillars. However, having different names, Jachin and Boaz, they must have been regarded as two different entities, or, as in the case of Amenhotep III's colossi, the two aspects of man. Although Islam, like Judaism, forbids image making, the Holy Qur'an states that King Solomon had jinn (supernatural creatures) working for him who "do for him whatever he desires of niches and statues" (34:13).

The ancient Egyptians believed that each person has two spiritual elements, the *ka* and the *ba*. They also believed that the living must help the dead in their afterlife journey by remembering them and keeping their names remembered. That is why, desiring to be eternally remembered by the living, Amenhotep III built these two great colossi in front of his temple.

The Colossi of Memnon are two massive stone statues of the pharaoh Amenhotep III, standing since 1350 BCE, representing his eternal soul. They are made from blocks of quartzite sandstone, which was quarried at El-Gabal el-Ahmar, near modern Cairo, and transported upstream to Thebes. Their original function was to stand guard at the entrance to the memorial temple. The colossi depict Amenhotep III in a seated position, his hands resting on his knees and his gaze facing east toward the river. Two shorter figures are carved into the front throne alongside his legs; these are his wife Tiye and mother, Mutemwiya. The modern names of the colossi are derived from Memnon, a hero of the Trojan War, a king of Ethiopia who led his armies from Africa into Asia Minor to help defend the beleaguered city but was slain by Achilles. *Memnon,* whose name means "the steadfast" or "the resolute," was said to be the son of Eos, the goddess of dawn. He was associated with the colossi because the northern statue was reported to ring at dawn. In 27 BCE, a large earthquake reportedly shattered it, making it collapse from the waist up and cracking the lower half. Following its rupture, the remaining lower half was reputed to ring on various occasions—always

The two Memnon statues at the entrance
of Amenhotep III's mortuary temple in western Thebes

within an hour or two of sunrise, usually right at dawn. The legend of the "Vocal Memnon"—the luck that hearing it was reputed to bring, and the reputation of the statue's oracular powers—became known outside of Egypt, and a constant stream of visitors, including several Roman emperors, came to marvel at the statues.

Given the similarities among luxurious materials used to build both Amenhotep III's and Solomon's temples, the sheer amount of effort required to physically construct such monumental buildings, and the apparent likeness in layout and design elements, we must pause to consider the source of these affinities.

SOLOMON AND TYRE

Can Solomon's Temple be regarded as a fairy tale invented by the biblical scribes? I don't think so. I believe that King Solomon *did* rule a great empire that extended between northern Syria and the borders of Egypt. I also believe that King Solomon *did* build a great Temple, as the Bible says. However, I do not agree either with dating Solomon to the tenth century BCE or with locating Solomon's Temple in Jerusalem. Since archaeologists have been looking in the wrong time and location, they have not been able to find the evidence.

Nevertheless, it is known that Amenhotep III established a small Egyptian shrine for his military force in the city of Jerusalem, which must have been in the same area where the Jews later built their temple.

Studying the relationship between Phoenicia and Solomon and comparing it to the relationship between Phoenicia and Egypt proves useful. Let us first examine the biblical account of how King Solomon built his Temple in Jerusalem, with the help of the Phoenician Hiram, king of Tyre, who sent him both cedar wood and technical workers:

When Hiram king of Tyre heard that Solomon had been anointed king to succeed his father David, he sent his envoys to Solomon, because he had always been on friendly terms with David. Solomon sent back his message to Hiram: "You know that because of the wars waged against my father David from all sides, he could not build a temple for the Name of the LORD his God. . . . But now the LORD my God has given me rest on every side. . . . I intend, therefore, to build a temple for the name of the LORD my God. . . . So give orders that cedars of Lebanon be cut for me. My men will work with yours, and I will pay you for your men whatever wages you set. . . ."

When Hiram heard Solomon's message, he was greatly pleased. . . . So Hiram sent word to Solomon: "I have received the message you sent me and will do all you want in providing the cedar." (1 Kings 5:1–8)

Following that, Solomon sent for a skilled Phoenician craftsman, named Huram, or Hiram, asking him to come to Jerusalem and supervise the building operation (1 Kings 7:13–14).

During this period in the tenth century BCE, the Phoenician city of Tyre was still an important source of the cedar wood that was needed to establish a major building like Solomon's Temple.

The land of the Phoenicians was an ancient civilization composed of independent city-states. The Phoenicians were a great maritime people who had developed a high level of skill in shipbuilding and were able to navigate the waters of the Mediterranean Sea. In ancient times, the land's abundant forests afforded the choicest lumber, particularly to its neighbors, especially Egypt.

As we have seen, the biblical text makes it clear that Solomon received much aid from Hiram in constructing his buildings. It is also believed that Solomon's Temple was built according to Phoenician design, in the same manner as Tyre's temple of Melqart. Both were surrounded by courts and had two pillars. Herodotus, the Greek historian, visited Tyre in the fifth century BCE. His description of the temple to Heracles is identified with the temple of Melqart. Herodotus writes, "The sanctuary was richly furnished, there were many votive offerings, and I noticed two pillars: one of pure gold and one of an emerald stone of such size as to shine by night" (Herodotus 2.44).

However, we have no historical sources, either in Tyre itself or in any of the neighboring countries, that mention Hiram as a king of Tyre. Our only nonbiblical source for Hiram comes from Josephus. Flavius Josephus, the Jewish historian who died at the end of the first century CE, claimed to have his sources of Phoenician records about King Hiram from two authors called Dius and Menander of Ephesus (Josephus, *Antiquities of the Jews,* 8.5.3). Josephus related that the construction of Solomon's Temple began in the twelfth year of Hiram's reign. But again, while Hiram is said to have reigned between 969 and 936 BCE, or between 980 and 947 BCE, no source outside the Bible mentions him except Josephus. Even the so-called Tomb of Hiram, located about six kilometers southeast of Tyre, was established much later, during the Persian period, about four hundred years after Hiram's presumed death.

Furthermore, in recent years, historians have begun to doubt the validity of Josephus's account, which was intended to prove the historicity of the Hebrew Bible. H. Jacob Katzenstein, author of *The History of Tyre,* writes: "Although Josephus speaks about copies of letters exchanged between Hiram, king of Tyre, and King Solomon, he does not give any quotation of these letters. At the same time, Eupolemus (the Jewish-Hellenistic author) quotes (!) some letters exchanged between Solomon and Hiram; they are, of course, not real letters, but the creation of Eupolemus's pen, based upon biblical material."[11]

Katzenstein also suggests that Josephus may have found his source in the fact that in the eleventh and twelfth years of his reign, Hiram built temples to Melqart and Astarte in Tyre and that Josephus applied these numbers to the date of building the Temple in Jerusalem. On the basis of a correlation with Babylonian and Assyrian chronology, another scholar contends that Josephus's data for the Tyrian and Hebrew kings are unreliable.[12]

The Amarna letters throw some light on the biblical account, which states: "King Solomon gave twenty towns in Galilee to Hiram king of Tyre, because Hiram had supplied him with all the cedar and juniper and gold he wanted" (1 Kings 9:11). However, in the Amarna letters, the name of Tyre's king is not Hiram but Abimilichi. In letter no. 99, in the Berlin Museum, Abimilichi asked the king to "give the city of Huzu to his servant [himself]." In another letter, no. 29, which is to be found in the British Museum, the king of Tyre indicated that another city had been placed under his control: "And now the city Zarbitu is to be guarded by the city of Tyre for the king, my Lord."

Some scholars have noticed that although Solomon's Temple has some features that could be similar to the Phoenician temples, it does also have similar features to other, non-Phoenician temples, like the Egyptian temple of Hatshepsut at Deir el-Bahri at Luxor, while its general form reminds one of Egyptian sanctuaries. Others have observed that, like Egyptian temples, Solomon's Temple is said to have had cherubim figures all over the building, even in the Holy of Holies, in violation of the divine prohibition against making graven images.

EGYPT AND TYRE

While no historical evidence has been found to confirm the biblical account regarding Tyre's relations with David and Solomon during the tenth century BCE, we find conclusive historical evidence to confirm these relations for Tuthmosis III and Amenhotep III.

Trade and friendship between Egypt and Phoenicia started very early, from the time of the Old Kingdom and the builders of the pyramids, and lasted three thousand years. Specifically, Egypt imported much wood from Tyre, proven by the modern uncovering of two cedar boats for the king's use in the afterlife buried beside the Great Pyramid of Khufu. It is known that Egypt and Tyre traded oils as well.

When Tuthmosis III invaded Syria, he incorporated Phoenicia into the Egyptian empire, holding it until about 1400 BCE. After that, Egypt used Canaan as a buffer against rival empires further north, such as Mitanni. Canaan also became a source of revenue through taxes, tribute, and trade. During this period, Egypt stationed small garrisons in major towns, like Jerusalem, and created administrative centers, like that in Beth She'an. These centers had buildings with distinctive Egyptian architecture and were inscribed with hieroglyphs.

From the time of Tuthmosis III on, Egypt had very close associations with all Phoenician cities, especially Tyre. Tuthmosis III's fifth, sixth, and seventh campaigns were directed against the Phoenician cities in the Levant and against Qadesh in northern Syria. According to his annals, in his Asiatic campaign of years 22–24, Tuthmosis III marched north through Tyre on his way to Qadesh.

Although Egypt's hold on the Levant was weakened after the death of Tuthmosis III, relations with Tyre remained very strong during the reign of Amenhotep III. According to Katzenstein, during the reigns of Amenhotep III and Akhenaten, "Tyre was Egypt's faithful ally. The city, which served occasionally as an anchorage-ground for the Egyptian army (EA 155:70), was one of the most important cities of the Phoenician Hanseatic League. As Tyre was the southern Phoenician coastal town nearest to Egypt and as its interests were pro-Egyptian, it became both a factor and an objective in the struggle for power between Egypt and her enemies, open and covert, in Western Asia."[13]

For example, King Abimilichi of Tyre sent a letter to the Egyptian king asking for his support in his conflict with Sidon. Abimilichi, whose name means "my father is king," held the rank of prince of Tyre around 1347 BCE. He is known to be the author of ten letters to the

Egyptian pharaoh. In letter EA 147, King Akhenaten confirmed him as ruler of Tyre upon the death of his father, and in EA 149, he referred to him with the rank *rabisu* (general).

In one of his letters to the Egyptian king, Abimilichi says:

> To the king, my lord, my god, my Sun: Message of Abi-Milku, your servant. I fall at the feet of the king, my lord, 7 times and 7 times. I am the dirt under the sandals of the king, my lord. My lord is the Sun who comes forth over all lands day by day, according to the way (of being) the sun, his gracious father, who gives life by his sweet breath and returns with his north wind; who establishes the entire land in peace, by the power of his arm: ha-pa-si; who gives forth his cry in the sky like Baal, and all land is frightened at his cry.
>
> The servant herewith writes to his lord that he heard the gracious messenger of the king who came to his servant, and the sweet breath that came forth from the mouth of the king. . . . When the king, my lord, said ku-na "(Prepare) before a large army" then the servant said to his lord: ia-a-ia-ia ("Yes, yes, yes"). . . . Zimredda, the king of Sidon, writes daily to the rebel Arizu . . . about every word he has heard from Egypt. I herewith write to my lord, and it is good that he knows.[14]

From the same period of Amenhotep III and Akhenaten, the Amarna letters include some letters from Jerusalem sent by a Canaanite ruler named Abdi-Heba. He states that he is a "soldier for the king, my lord," and requests that the Egyptian monarch send him a messenger and some military men to help resist his enemies. Like Abimilichi in the letter above, he says that he "falls at the feet of my lord the king, seven times and seven times," a stock phrase that conveys his faithfulness to his Egyptian suzerain. Abdi-Heba also reveals that he was not the heir to the throne but was given the throne of Jerusalem by the

Egyptian king himself. He goes on to say that for this reason he will always be a faithful vassal of his Egyptian lord.

Despite the lack of mention of the king of Tyre in sources besides the Bible, it is obvious that Amenhotep III and his successor Akhenaten maintained a solid relationship with the Phoenicians. If we accept Solomon as Amenhotep III, we can see where the biblical scribes may have drawn their material.

I have identified Solomon as the pharaoh Amenhotep III and have shown that archaeologists have been looking in the wrong location for Solomon's temple, which shares similarities with Amenhotep III's mortuary temple in western Thebes. Now that we have found Solomon's Temple in Egypt, we can look for the architect, known as Hiram Abiff, who designed and supervised its construction.

18

Secrets of the Architect

THE BIBLICAL ACCOUNT STATES that Hiram was king of Tyre during the reigns of both David and Solomon. After David's death, Hiram maintained his alliance with David's son and successor. He offered his help to build his Temple in Jerusalem and sent Solomon workmen, cedar wood, and gold for the construction. The Bible also states that the king of Tyre sent an architect to superintend the construction of the Temple (2 Chronicles 2:13). Hiram the architect, the Bible says, was a son of a widow of the tribe of Dan, one of the twelve tribes of Israel, and of a Tyrian father (2 Chronicles 2:14). This architect was, like the king, named Hiram. (Although both the king of Tyre and his namesake, the architect, are named Hiram, in some cases the Bible refers to both of them by other names, such as "Huram"; 2 Chronicles 4:11–12.)

Translations of 2 Chronicles 2:13 differ on the architect's exact name. In Hebrew it is *Huram abi*. *Abi* in Hebrew means "my father," and the King James Version renders this verse: "And now I have sent a cunning man, endued with understanding, of Huram my father's." But the New International Version, like most modern translations, renders *abi* as part of a proper name: "I am sending you Huram-Abi, a man of great skill." The Masonic tradition agrees that Abi (Abiff in the Masonic version) is part of his name.

Freemasons are perfectly correct in refusing to adopt the translation of the English version, and in preserving, after the example of Luther, the word *Abif* as an appellative, surname, or title of honor and distinction bestowed upon the relief builder of the Temple.[1]

HIRAM RESURRECTED

Masonic tradition has introduced other material about Hiram Abiff that is not found in the Bible or in any other source:

> The legend tells us that one day, whilst worshipping the Grand Architect of the Universe (GAOTU) within the Holy of Holies, Hiram was attacked by three ruffians (called "Jubela," "Jubelo," and "Jubelum" and known collectively as "The Juwes") who demanded the "Master's word," that is, the secret name of God.
>
> The first ruffian, named Jubela, struck Hiram across the throat with a 24 inch gauge. The second ruffian, named Jubelo, struck Hiram's breast, over the heart, with a square. The third ruffian, named Jubelum, struck Hiram upon the forehead with a gavel, whereupon Hiram fell dead. His blood, therefore, was shed within the temple.
>
> Hiram, having been killed, was carried out the East gate of the Temple and buried outside Jerusalem on Mount Moriah.
>
> Early the following morning, King Solomon visited the temple and found the workmen in confusion because no plan had been made for the day's work. Fearing evil had befallen Hiram, King Solomon sent out twelve Fellow Craft Masons to look for Hiram. King Solomon himself accompanied the three who journeyed towards the East.
>
> Having finally located the grave of Hiram, Solomon and his fellow Masons exhumed the body. A search was made for the Master's word (the Name of God), but all that was found was the letter "G."

Finding the word lost, a lament went up: "O Lord, my God, is there no help for the widow's son?"

Solomon finally raised Hiram from the dead, by using the third degree grip of the Master Mason, the five points of fellowship . . . and by uttering in Hiram's ear the phrase "MA-Ha-Bone." Nevertheless, although the Masonic account states that Hiram Abiff was raised from the dead, he did not return to his previous life on earth, but was, like the risen Christ, "ushered into a more glorious existence."[2]

HISTORICAL EVIDENCE

As in the case of Hiram, king of Tyre, and of Solomon's house and Temple in Jerusalem, modern archaeology has found no evidence to confirm the existence of Hiram Abiff in history. Nevertheless, if the Masonic information about Hiram Abiff represents a lost ancient tradition, as I believe it does, we might be able to establish the true identity of the great builder and know when and where he lived. For the Masons believe that Hiram Abiff was, like Jesus Christ, a redeemer.

In Masonic literature, the first mention of their Hiramic legend, including the murder, the discovery of his body, and raising him from the dead, occurred in 1730, in Samuel Richard's *Masonry Dissected*. If this account is not found in the Bible, what was its source?

The Masonic fraternity, like the Rosicrucians in Germany and the Netherlands, might have had an ancient tradition going back to Gnostic groups that appeared in Alexandria in the first few centuries CE. Although the Gnostics' remnants were consistently repressed by the Roman Catholic Church during the Middle Ages, western Gnosticism continued to exist in various underground versions. After the Protestant Reformation and the advent of religious tolerance in the seventeenth and eighteenth centuries, Gnosticism began to resurface in forms including the Masons and Rosicrucians.

The most important part of Masonic tradition which could point to the real historical account of Solomon and his architect, is the account that talks about the killing of Hiram Abiff and his resurrection from the dead by the king. If my argument above is correct, the place where Hiram Abiff was resurrected was not in Jerusalem, but in Egypt.

Up to the first century CE, when Jesus Christ is believed to have been risen from the dead, no nation other than Egypt believed in or practiced resurrection. Neither the Israelites nor the Jews believed that their dead could be resurrected. There is no afterlife in the Old Testament: the dead go to Sheol, a place of darkness to which all go, cast off from life and from God. Through much of the Old Testament period, it was believed that all went to this one place, whether human or animal, whether righteous or wicked. No one could escape Sheol, which was thought to be down in the lowest parts of the earth (Deuteronomy 32:22; 1 Samuel 28:11–15).

The soul or spirit is also not mentioned in the Old Testament. The Hebrew word *nephesh,* which has sometimes been translated to mean *soul,* was always used in the Old Testament to indicate the vitality or life force of a person. For example, Genesis 46:18, in the King James Version, uses the word *soul:* "These are the sons of Zilpah, whom Laban gave to Leah his daughter, and these she bare unto Jacob, even sixteen souls." The same verse was correctly translated by the New International Version to indicate *person:* "These were the children born to Jacob by Zilpah, whom Laban had given to his daughter Leah—sixteen in all."

Later, in around the seventh century BCE, the prophet Isaiah talks, for the first time, about the hope that the dead could be born again: "Your dead will live; their bodies will rise. You who dwell in the dust, wake up and shout for joy. Your dew is like the dew of the morning; the earth will give birth to her dead" (Isaiah 26:19).

In Mesopotamia, people hoped to overcome death, but they did not believe in the resurrection of the dead. Rather, they were hoping to find a remedy that could give them eternal youth. In the Babylonian epic *Gilgamesh,* which is about four thousand years old, Gilgamesh asks Utnapishtim, the only survivor of a mythological flood, about the secret of immortality. Utnapishtim directs him to a plant that will renew his youth, but Gilgamesh fails to return with it to his home city.

In India, Hindus believe in reincarnation, but they say that if you have bad karma and a life full of sins, you have to take rebirth again and again. Buddhists believe in a cycle of death and rebirth called *samsara.* Through the accumulation of good karma and eventual enlightenment, they hope to escape samsara and achieve nirvana, an end to the suffering of reincarnation.

Only in Egypt, from its early history on, do we find a belief in life after death. To the Egyptians, dying was not the end, but merely an event that they had to pass through to reach a new stage of existence and join the rest of the dead, who shared the universe with the gods and the living. They also believed that a person's body would continue to play a vital part in his or her existence after physical death, which is why they spent so much time figuring out how to preserve dead bodies.

The Egyptians believed that humans have two dimensions: one physical, which perishes after death, and the other spiritual, that is, eternal. For this reason, they worked hard to preserve the body of the dead through mummification and burial in a secure tomb protected by magical spells from the funerary texts known as the Book of the Dead. They also believed that one day in the future, the soul would be able to return to the body and resurrect the dead person. For the Egyptians, the personality was created at the moment of birth, but the soul was an eternal entity inhabiting a mortal vessel. When the vessel failed and the person's body died, the soul went on to another plane of existence where, if it was justified by the gods, it would live forever in a paradise that was a mirror image of its earthly existence. Mortuary rituals were carefully observed because each aspect of the soul had to be addressed in order for it to continue on its way to eternity.

Nobody believes that Hiram Abiff, following his resurrection, went home and came back to work the following day; resurrection here means going through the ritual performed by the Egyptians on their dead. Egyptians believed that, in order for a person to survive the afterlife, his or her body had to be mummified by removing all moisture from it, leaving only a dried form that would not decay, and wrapping it in strips of linen. Then the priests, having placed the mummified body in a standing position, performed the ritual of "opening the mouth" so that the dead person could eat and drink again in the afterlife.

Scene from the tomb of Tutankhamun illustrating
the ritual of opening the mouth

However, as with the resurrection of Jesus Christ, the Egyptians did not believe that the dead person would go back to his or her earthly home, but rather that the soul would live eternally with the gods. This is exactly what the Masons mean when talking about Hiram Abiff's resurrection.

Freemasons also believe that Hiram Abiff was a healer and philosopher whose followers kept his teaching for many centuries after his death. It was they who later became known as the Gnostics of the early Christian era. The Masons also relate Hiram Abiff to the philosophy of Hermes Trismegistus (Hermes Thrice Greatest), the Greek name for Egyptian Tehut, god of knowledge, including healing, alchemy, magic, Kabbalah, and astrology.

Strangely enough, it was this nonbiblical information, preserved by the Masons, that pointed to the historical identity of Hiram Abiff and to the location of Solomon's Temple.

Now we can identify the character of the architect, starting with his name. Although the name of the architect was written in four different ways—*Hiram, Huram, Horam,* and *Hirum*—we can see that in all these cases, only the vowels change, while the consonants remain the same: H R M. The true name of the architect can be easily identified when we add the letter S at the end—HRMS. The architect was later identified with Hermes because of his philosophy.

As for *Abiff,* it is related to the Hebrew *abi,* which, as we have seen, means "my father." So, the name of the architect who supervised the building of Solomon's Temple relates him to his father. This is exactly what we will find when we look at the great architect who built the mortuary temple for Amenhotep III in Egypt.

AMENHOTEP THE ARCHITECT

Known also as Huy, Amenhotep, the great architect who supervised the building of the Temple for Amenhotep III, was born around year 38 of Tuthmosis III, around 1440 BCE. He belonged to a humble family from the ancient city of Athribis in the eastern Delta, near modern Banha. His father was called Habu and his mother Idit. Following his education at the local temple, the son of Habu worked as a scribe in local government through the reign of Amenhotep II and Tuthmosis IV. When his namesake, Amhenhotep III, sat on the throne, he was called to join the royal court in his early fifties.

Under Amenhotep III, the son of Habu started his official life as a scribe in the court, but soon after he was able to succeed to a higher rank, eventually becoming the chief of public works. In this position, he supervised the construction of many important monuments for the king in Karnak, Luxor, and Thebes. As the king favored him, he had an extraordinarily distinguished career, holding the positions of chief architect, chief scribe, and secretary in charge of recruiting, as well as steward to Queen Sitamun. He was also in charge of recruiting the hundreds of thousands of builders employed to design and construct the pharaoh's extensive building program, and it was he who supervised the development of Amenhotep III's projects, including his royal palace at Malqata and the mortuary temple nearby.

On his statue, the son of Habu gave details of his work at the court of Amenhotep III, explaining how he received the secret knowledge of Tehut or Thoth: "I was appointed to be inferior king's scribe; I was introduced into the divine book, I beheld the excellent thing of Thoth (Hermes); I was equipped with their secrets; I opened all their [passages?]; one [the king] took counsel with me on all their matters."[3]

Amenhotep's father Habu is sometimes identified in later texts with "the living herald Apis"—that is, the Apis bull—while his mother, Idit, is referred to as "Hathor-Idit, the justified, the mother of the helpful God who issued from her on this beautiful day, the 11th of Phamenoth, in her name 'rejoicing.'" In addition to the divinization of his mortal parents, Amenhotep is often characterized as the son of Amun or Thoth.[4]

So it was Amenhotep, the namesake not of Hiram, king of Tyre, but

Amenhotep, son of Habu, the great architect of Amenhotep III

of Amenhotep III, king of Egypt, who built both the royal palace and the Temple. The son of Habu, the great architect, was allowed to erect his own statues in the holy domain of the temple of Amun-Re at Karnak and build his own funerary temple near the royal temple on the west bank of the Nile. He also held some important titles: "He had an extraordinarily distinguished career under Amenhotep III, holding the positions of chief architect . . . chief scribe and secretary in charge of recruit."[5]

THE SON OF HABU
AND HIS CONNECTION TO MOSES

The son of Habu is believed to have lived at the same time as when Moses was in Egypt, before the Israelite Exodus. A later Egyptian account indicates that Amenhotep, son of Habu, was even involved in the conflict between Moses and his followers and the Egyptian establishment. Although we do not find any account of Moses and the Israelites recorded in contemporary Egyptian records, it seems that many of its details have survived in popular traditions, which retained the story for more than ten centuries before they were finally recorded.

Manetho, an Egyptian priest of the third century BCE, wrote a history of Egypt in Greek to be placed in the library of Alexandria, during the reign of the king Ptolemy II Philadelphus. Manetho included the story of Moses in his *Egyptiaca*. Although Manetho's original account was lost, Flavius Josephus, the Jewish historian of the first century CE, preserved the story. Josephus says: "This king [Amenophis] states, wishing to be granted . . . a vision of the gods, communicated his desire to his namesake, Amenophis, son of Papis [son of Habu], whose wisdom and knowledge of the future were regarded as marks of divinity. This namesake replied that he would be able to see the gods if he purged the entire country of lepers and other polluted persons and sent them to work on the stone quarries to the east of the Nile, segregated from the rest of the Egyptians. They included, he adds, some of the learned priests, who were afflicted with leprosy."[6] Josephus goes on to say: "It remains for me to say a word about Manetho and Moses. The Egyptians, who regard that man as remarkable, indeed divine, wish to claim him as one of themselves."[7]

As he was objecting to Manetho's account, Josephus could not have invented the story of Moses being an Egyptian, parts of which are reported also by other writers. Although Egypti n contemporary records do not mention the name *Moses,* they do give an account of another monotheistic leader who lived at the same time: Amenhotep IV, son of Amenhotep III, who later changed his name to Akhenaten. As his name was struck out of official records and forbidden to be mentioned after his death, popular accounts must have referred to him by another name—Moses?

If we try to understand why the son of Habu warned the king about Moses, we have to go back about four years before the death of the wise man, to the date when Amenhotep III associated his son with him on the throne as a coregent. At that point a fierce conflict began between the priests of Amun and Amenhotep III, which forced the king to ask his son to leave Thebes and live in Amarna. According to Josephus, quoting Manetho, the son of Habu, who foretold major trouble for the royal family, warned the king before committing suicide. "Manetho further states that the seer [Son of Habu] killed himself, because he foresaw the anger of the gods and the fate in store for Egypt, leaving to the king his prediction in writing."[8]

Eventually, the son of Habu's prophecy proved to be right: the Amarna rule eventually led to the end of the Thutmosid Dynasty, which was succeeded by the Ramessids' Nineteenth Dynasty.

THE SON OF HABU'S DEATH

If we are to believe Manetho's account as quoted by Josephus, Amenhotep, son of Habu, must have committed suicide, fearing the gods' anger, when he was about eighty. Although his tomb has not been found, it is generally believed that he was buried in western Thebes, probably somewhere in Qurnet El Murnai.

After his death, in year 31 of Amenhotep III, the son of Habu's reputation grew, and he was revered for his teachings as a philosopher. Like his predecessor, Imhotep, he was also revered as a healer and eventually worshipped as a god of healing. Imhotep was the chief architect to the Egyptian king Djoser (Zoser), who ruled 2630–2611 BCE, and was responsible for the world's first known monumental stone building, the Step Pyramid at Saqqara. He is also the first architect to be known by name.

> Son of Habu, was of great importance and was honoured for his contribution by Pharaoh himself, who built Huy [son of Habu] a statue in the Temple of Amun at Karnak, a great honour and a mortuary temple in western Thebes which was of as much magnificence as the Pharaohs' that surrounded it. One command that came from the king states the importance of his mortuary temple/cult: "Hear the command which is given to furnish the ka-chapel of the hereditary prince, the royal scribe, Amenhotep, called Huy, [Son of Habu], whose excellence is extolled, in order to perpetuate his ka-chapel with slaves, male and female, forever, son to son, heir to heir, in order that none trespass upon it forever."[9]

THE DEIFICATION OF THE SON OF HABU

On his seated statue at Karnak, now in the Egyptian Museum in Cairo, the son of Habu is depicted as an aged man, sitting with his hands on his knees in a pose of prayer (see page 167). This statue, in gray granite, was found in front of the north face of the seventh pylon and was originally designed to act as an intermediary between the living and the gods. The inscription says: "Ye people of Karnak, ye who wish to see Amon, come to me! I shall report your petitions. [For] I am indeed the messenger of this god. [The king] has appointed me to report the works of the Two Lands. Speak to me the 'offering spell' and invoke my name daily, as is done to one who has taken a vow."[10]

The son of Habu was a deified human, and thus he was depicted only in human form, with several surviving statues portraying him as a scribe, a young man, and an older man. His cult was started in the area of Thebes, and a funerary temple to him, next to that of Amenhotep III, was constructed during his lifetime. This was clearly an exceptional privilege, as it was the only private cult temple to be built among the royal monuments in the area. Gradually, especially after his prophecy proved to be right, his cult spread all over Egypt, and he continued to be worshipped centuries after his death. During the Ptolemaic Dynasty, he was associated with Asclepius, and a chapel was dedicated to him on the third terrace of the temple of Hatshepsut at Deir el-Bahri.

Asclepius was a hero and god in ancient Greek religion and mythology who represented the healing aspects of the medical art. The rod of Asclepius, a snake-entwined staff, remains the symbol of medicine today. The physicians and attendants who served this god were known as the *therapeutai* (healers). As we shall see, the healers who appear later in Egypt early in the first century CE were followers of the son of Habu.

Amenhotep, son of Habu,

was often worshiped alongside his fellow deified architect and healer Imhotep, even surpassing him in popularity. In a hymn inscribed on the temple of Ptah at Karnak, it is said of son of Habu and Imhotep that they have a single "body" and a single *ba,* "soul" or "manifestation,'" as if Amenhotep son of Habu were a veritable reincarnation of his colleague who had lived one thousand years prior. Spells, Pleyte 167 of the Book of the Dead, is labeled as having been found by "the king's chief scribe Amenhotep the son of Habu. . . . He used it for him [the king] as protection for his body. Amenhotep son of Habu and Imhotep are [also] mentioned in the Papyrus Boulaq (first century CE) as welcoming the soul of the deceased: 'Your soul will go to the royal scribe and chief of the recruits Amenhotep; your soul will be united with Imhotep. . . . You will feel like a son in the house of his father.'"[11]

This great architect, philosopher, and healer is depicted as a scribe, often with palette and scroll, corpulent and somewhat older, with a fuller hairstyle or wig than the standard kind, a short beard, and often a long apron. Votive inscriptions from a Ptolemaic chapel behind the upper mortuary temple of Hatshepsut at Deir el-Bahri show that he was still worshipped in the second century CE, more than fifteen hundred years after his death.

Like that of Imhotep, the architect of the great mortuary monuments of Djoser, the memory of this Amenhotep survived for many centuries. He was reckoned as one of the sages of Egypt, and sayings attributed to him were still current in the Ptolemaic period. Because of his wisdom and his alleged ability to foresee coming events, he was held to be of divine nature. Finally, under one of the successors of Alexander the Great—probably Ptolemy VIII Euergetes II, about 140 BCE—he was deified and henceforth worshiped as a god.[12]

Votary text inscribed on a statue was dedicated to the son of Habu by a daughter of King Psamtik of the Twenty-Sixth Dynasty. Although medicine had not been one of Amenhotep's many accomplishments, his ability to intercede on behalf of the suffering had magical qualities and was therefore considered to be strong medicine: "Oh noble Amenhotep son of Hapu, true of voice. Come, good physician I suffer from my eyes. May you cause that I be healthy at once."[13]

A Greek votive text from Deir el-Bahri dating from the Ptolemaic period says, "I enquire of the great god Amenhotep. He replied that a fever was in the body of Teos and that one might give him two Syrian figs, watered from the evening to the morning."[14]

Even later, in the Roman period, the son of Habu was still remembered in association with Imhotep: "The learned ones praise god for you [Imhotep], Foremost among them your brother, who loves you, whom you love, Amenhotep son of Hapu. He abides with you, He parts not from you; Your bodies form a single one, Your bas receive the things you love, Brought you by your son, Caesar Augustus."[15]

"A text dating from the time of Tiberius [who ruled 14–37 CE] refers to him as the 'youthful repetition of Ptah. . . . You give a child to the sterile; you release a man from his enemy; you know the hearts of men and what is inside; fill up what was found destroyed.'"[16]

THE SON OF HABU, HIRAM, AND HERMES

Always proud of his knowledge, the son of Habu claimed to know the secrets of Thoth, identified with the Greek Hermes, god of wisdom and knowledge. Maybe that is why the architect who is said by the Bible to have supervised the building of Solomon's Temple became known as Hiram or HRMS (a short form of Hermes).

Hermes Trismegistus, teacher of theology and philosophy, became a mysterious figure in the Greco-Roman world. He was seen as an all-knowing sage, and his mythic attributes derived from the Egyptian Thoth. Thoth, or Tehuti, was the Egyptian god of knowledge who invented writing, made the first measurement of time, and gave order to civil and religious life. From the dawn of their historical times, as early as 3000 BCE, the Egyptians regarded Thoth as the master of all speech and communication and thus as the mediator between gods and humans. Originally Thoth was worshipped in his principal cult location, called Hermopolis by the Greeks, near modern Amarna in Upper Egypt. Later, during the Ptolemaic rule in Alexandria, Thoth was known as Hermes, the Greek god who was also identified with the *logos* of philosophy.

Looked upon by the ancient Egyptians as the First Intelligencer, the embodiment of the Universal Mind, or Thoth, Hermes Trismegistus was believed to be the master of all arts and sciences, perfect in all crafts, Ruler of the Three Worlds, Scribe of the Gods, and Keeper of the Books of Life. The appellation *Trismegistus,* "Thrice Greatest," was given to him because he was considered to be the greatest of all philosophers, the greatest of all priests, and the greatest of all kings.

It is also believed that before his death, Hermes entrusted to his chosen successors the sacred Book of Thoth. This work contained the secret key to his writings. Nevertheless, this book was lost, and all that is now known of its contents is that its pages were covered with strange hieroglyphic figures and symbols, which gave to those acquainted with their use unlimited power over the spirits of the air and the subterranean divinities, as well as the key to immortality.

Although originally Thoth was a god, eventually some humans who were able to receive the secret of divine knowledge became identified with him, including Imhotep and the son of Habu.

Hermes was not just a sage; he was believed to be ruler of the world, king of all knowledge, and father and teacher of all. Yet he was mortal. It is said that when he died, like Hiram Abiff and the son of Habu, he was resurrected and ascended to the heavens to become a link between the transcendent God and his creation.

Hermes Trismegistus is the prototypical teacher of Egyptian wisdom. In Hermes's doctrine, man possesses two souls. One has a share in the intelligible world, and the other stands in relation to the stars; it is subject to their periodic movements and influences the body by means of these movements. This soul descends from the stars into the human body and is freed from the body at death. Then the soul returns to the stars, now able to behold the divine. But even when it is still in man, the soul that shares in the intelligible can ascend to the gods and is not subject to destiny. With this soul, man can liberate himself through knowledge of God and the world.

A key tenet of Hermetic belief is the unity of the cosmos and the sympathy and interconnection between all things. As in the ancient Egyptian belief, man not only is a physical body but also has a spiritual dimension, which is part of the Universal Spirit. The Hermetic texts contain a conversation among Hermes, Asclepius, Ammon, and Tat about this belief. It is said, "All is part of one, or one is all." This means that individual entities have no essence or eternal being of their own, but as part of the One they become immortal. Man, who is essentially spirit, wishes in the end to be freed from his corporeality through death, to ascend into the spiritual realm.

Hermes Trismegistus, *by Giovanni di Stefano,*
in the floor pavement at Italy's Siena Cathedral

Like the son of Habu, Hermes Trismegistus was traditionally believed to have lived at about the same time as Moses.[17] The floor of the cathedral at Siena has a famous portrait of the sage, dated 1488, and attributed to the sculptor Giovanni di Stefano. The legend beneath the central figure reads, "Hermes Mercurius Trismegistus, the contemporary of Moses."

As King Akhenaten, whom I have identified as Moses, was the first one in history to recognize the unity of the spiritual being, we can only guess how this idea later become the cornerstone of Hermetic belief.

THE *HERMETICA*

The written texts containing the secret knowledge of Hermes, composed by different authors over hundreds of years, became known collectively as the *Hermetica*. Thus Hermeticism is a religious, philosophical, and esoteric tradition based upon the writings attributed to Hermes Trismegistus. According to the third-century church father Clement of Alexandria, the *Hermetica* represent Egyptian religion, and identifying the history of Hermeticism means describing how the knowledge of this wise old Egyptian, Hermes, was passed down through the centuries, as well as the significance assigned to him and the development over time of the corpus of literature that was credited to him. The original number of Hermetic writings could have been considerable, but most of these texts were probably lost during the Catholic church's systematic destruction of what it regarded as heretical writings between the fourth and sixth centuries CE.

Later, when some of these texts were rediscovered, they greatly influenced Western cultural memory. In 1460, the ruler of Florence, Cosimo de' Medici, acquired several previously lost Hermetic texts that had been found in the Byzantine Empire, and they became known as the *Corpus Hermaticum* or the *Hermetica,* a set of seventeen short Greek texts. Two other, longer texts stand alone. The first is the *Asclepius,* preserved in a Latin translation dating probably from the third century CE. The second takes the form of a dialogue between Isis and Horus and has the unusual title of *Korē Kosmou,* which means "daughter of the world." Translated by Marsilio Ficino and others into Latin in 1463, the Hermetic books soon gained the attention of the intelligentsia all over Europe and led to an intellectual revolution during the Renaissance.

According to German Egyptologist Jan Assmann, the most important element in Hermetic tradition is the motif of revelation. Assmann believes that this motif is bound up with the motif of secrecy, for which reason it was encoded not in the letters of an alphabet, but in hieroglyphics, which were understood to be a medium of enciphering ideas independent of language. Hieroglyphic writing, in his view, can be read only by the initiated; thus the Hermetic traditions regard themselves as a nondiscursive philosophy communicated only through symbols.

Assmann regards initiation as the third main concept connected with the Hermetic traditions. This involves not only knowing the hieroglyphic code but also demonstrating that one is worthy of this knowledge. For the ancient Egyptians, knowledge was to be communicated only to the worthy, as it was connected with the special power ascribed to natural symbols.[18]

The library of Coptic texts discovered in 1945 at Nag Hammadi in Upper Egypt contained some previously unknown Hermetic texts from the fourth century, including *The Discourse on the Eighth and Ninth.*[19] It lists the prerequisites for the success of mystical vision. Hermes instructs his disciple regarding the step-by-step spiritual ascent to true knowledge. Truth and the path to beholding God cannot simply be learned, however, for there are appropriate intellectual and moral prerequisites, and adequate practice is needed. The first step has to do with distancing oneself from the world, with freedom from base physical drives. One must engage in pious practices and live according to the laws of God, thus fulfilling a necessary condition for mystic vision.

Only those who fear God can hope to be elevated in prayer into the divine Ogdoad, which leads to truth and wisdom.

HERMETIC MAGIC

Like Solomon, Hermes was involved in magic, and the Hermetic tradition refers to alchemy, magic, astrology, and related subjects. Magic, for the ancient Egyptians, was the harnessing of the powers of natural laws, conceived of as supernatural entities, in order to achieve certain goals. Magic is the power of using apparently supernatural forces to change the forms of things or influence events. The Egyptians believed that the divine word and magical energy could be used to turn concepts into reality. To the Egyptians, a world without magic was inconceivable.

They generally treated diseases according to the perceived cause: pragmatic means were adopted for conditions for which the cause was evident (such as the use of bone setting and surgery for trauma), whereas magic was used for more obscure complaints, which might be attributed to supernatural agents.

Hermes Trismegistus, and the natural-philosophical ideas ascribed to him, also belongs to the background in which alchemy arose in late antiquity. The oldest collections of chemical formulas are found in a group of papyri in Leiden and Stockholm. These papyri contain instructions on how to replicate silver, using code names to designate the materials required. Gold, or the Philosopher's Stone, is to be prepared from lead through a process in which the lead turns black, white, yellow, then red.

THE ART OF HEALING

At the same time, Hermes was considered to be the founding father of iatromathematics, a system based on the doctrine of cosmobiology, which relates particular mental and physical conditions to the positions of celestial bodies. The doctrine of the rule of the planets over humans and their body parts stresses this relationship: it specifies which planetary gods cause which ailments and lists the treatments indicated for curing or relieving them. Thus in the Hermetic tradition astrology was understood to be the key to medicine.

The son of Habu, deified as a god of wisdom and medicine, became identified with Asclepius, the god of medicine. According to the *Hermetica,* Asclepius (who has one of its treatises named after him) was one of two students of Hermes Trismegistus; the second was Hermes's own son, Tat. In the *Asclepius,* we learn that the Hermetic Asclepius is actually a descendant of the deified Asclepius-Imhotep. Asclepius was a skilled healer who could bring people back from the dead. Like the son of Habu and Hiram Abiff, Hermes Trismegistus was said to have been spiritually resurrected after his death: "Hermes, while wandering in a rocky and desolate place, gave himself over to meditation and prayer. Following the secret instruction of the *Temple,* he gradually freed his higher consciousness from the bondage of his bodily senses; and, thus released, his divine nature revealed to him the mysteries of the transcendental spheres. He beheld a figure, terrible and awe-inspiring. . . . Hermes was '*raised*' into the midst of this Divine Effulgence and the universe of material things faded from his consciousness."[20]

During Ptolemaic times, a cult had developed at the Temple of Hatshepsut at Deir el-Bahri that was dedicated to Amenhotep, son of Habu, on the upper terrace of the temple. During the reign of Ptolemy III Euergetes, in the second half of the third century BCE, a special room was constructed to house the patients. Here they left numerous graffiti on the walls, which date to the second century CE. Most of them were dedicated to Asclepius in association with Amenhotep, son of Habu.[21]

As well as being an architect, the man who built Solomon's Temple was a philosopher and a healer who was acquainted with magic and was spiritually resurrected after his death. Such a man could not have lived in Phoenician Tyre or Jerusalem in the tenth century BCE, nor could he have lived anywhere else other than Egypt. Historically, the account of Hiram Abiff could only fit one person: Amenhotep, son of Habu.

19

The Birth and Repression of Gnosticism

THE CULT OF AMENHOTEP, son of Habu, developed over time, to reach its zenith at the start of the first century CE. With the death of Cleopatra VII, the last of the Ptolemaic Dynasty, in 30 BCE, the rule of the pharaohs came to an end. From then onward Egypt was ruled by a prefect who was appointed by the Roman emperor and resided in Alexandria. Although pharaonic customs and traditions still continued under Roman rule, major developments took place, especially in religion. As the Romans stopped financing the temples except for the Serapeum in Alexandria, Egyptians felt lost, with no place to worship. However, as the religious establishment gradually died out, new popular organizations emerged.

THE THERAPEUTAE

Looking for spiritual salvation, a new group, the Therapeutae, emerged. The Therapeutae, "healers" or "attendants" (from the Greek *therapeuō*, "to heal" or "care for") are believed to have settled on the shores of Lake Mareotis near Alexandria. The only original account of this community is given in Philo's treatise *De vita contemplativa* (On the contemplative life).

Philo, a member of the flourishing Jewish community in Alexandria, was born around 15 BCE and died around 50 CE. He was influenced by the philosophy of Plato and attempted to reconcile pagan philosophy with the revelations of the Bible. His writings were recognized as having a close affinity with Christian ideas, and for this reason they were preserved and studied by the church.

The Therapeutae, according to Philo, were members of a contemplative community that embraced the simple life. On becoming members, they renounced the world completely, fleeing "without ever turning to look back, abandoning brothers, children, wives, parents. . . . They make settlements for themselves outside the walls, in gardens or in solitary places, seeking solitude."[1]

They left their possessions to their relatives or friends and went to live in encampments of individual huts: "They eat no costly food, but simple bread and, as a seasoning, salt. . . . Spring water was their only drink."[2] They began each day with prayers around daybreak. More prayers followed toward evening. The hours in between they devoted to reading the Hebrew Scriptures. "They philosophise and interpret allegorically their native code of laws, since they regard the words of the literal interpretation as symbols of a hidden nature revealed only in such figures of speech."[3] They also studied the writings of their Jewish forebears, founders of the sect, about the truths enshrined in these allegories.

Philo says that the Therapeutae spread out of Egypt to other nations so that "this sect is to be found in many parts of the civilized world." In Egypt itself it was "numerous throughout each of the districts called Nomes, and particularly around Alexandria."[4]

In his *Ecclesiastical History*, written in the early fourth century CE, Eusebius of Caesarea identified the Alexandrian Therapeutae as the first Christian community in Egypt: "So large was the body of believers, men and women alike . . . that Philo [of Alexandria] decided that he must record in writing their activities . . . in the work that he entitled *The Contemplative Life*." Eusebius insists upon the Christian nature of the Therapeutae: "These statements of Philo seem to me to refer plainly and unquestionably to members of our Church" (*Ecclesiastical History*, 2:17).

Eusebius stresses that Philo

describes the life of our ascetics with the greatest precision. . . . He says that they are called *Therapeutae* and their womenfolk *Therapeutrides* . . . either because like doctors they rid the souls of those who come to them from mortal sickness and so cure and heal them, or in view of their pure and sincere service and worship of God . . . because the title Christians was not yet in general use. . . . If anyone does not agree that what has been described is peculiar to the gospel way of life but thinks it applicable to other people too, he will surely be convinced by Philo's next paragraph, in which, if he is reasonable, he will find the evidence on this point beyond dispute:

"Having first laid down self-control as a foundation for the soul, they build the other virtues on it. None of them would take food or drink before sundown, as they hold that philosophy deserves daylight but darkness is good enough for bodily needs. So, to the one they assign the day, to the others a small part of the night. . . ."

These statements of Philo seem to me to refer plainly and unquestionably to members of our Church. But, if after this someone insists on denying it, he will surely abandon his scepticism and be convinced by still clearer evidences which cannot be found anywhere but in the religious practices of Christians who follow the gospel. For Philo states that among the people in question there are women also, most of them elderly spinsters who have remained single, not of necessity, like some priestesses of pagan cults, but of their own free will, through their passionate craving for wisdom. . . . Need I add to this an account of their meetings, or of the segregation of men and women living in the same place, or of the regular spiritual discipline still practised among us, especially during the commemoration of our Saviour's Passion, when it is our habit to abstain from food, spend the whole nights in prayer, and devote ourselves to the word of God? (*Ecclesiastical History, 2.17*)

There are indications that the Christian monastic movement, which appeared in its full form only in the third century CE, had its origins with the Therapeutae: "The ascetics . . . were recognized as a defined group within the Christian congregations as early as the end of the second century. . . . It has been held that the new Christian monasticism was a revival or development of the . . . Therapeutae described by Philo."[5]

Nevertheless, at this early stage of the Christian movement, we find no mention of the name of Jesus, and no account of his birth or crucifixion, but only his teachings regarding salvation. The first appearance of Jesus's name comes with Mark the evangelist, who has been viewed as the founder of the Egyptian Coptic Church and the first in the line of Alexandrian patriarchs. From the early days of the Christian church, confirmation of Mark's journey to Egypt was believed to be found in the New Testament: "She [the church] who is at Babylon, chosen together with you, sends you her greetings, and so does my son Mark" (1 Peter 5:13). "*Babylon* here can only be the Egyptian town of that name (in old Cairo). Peter went with Marcus to Egypt. . . . With Coptic and Roman Catholic authors, it is a received fact that the tidings of salvation were first brought to Egypt by Mark, the author of the second gospel."[6]

GNOSTIC CHRISTIANITY

Eventually the Therapeutae movement developed its doctrine, built on Hermetic teachings, and produced many books, including some gospels of Christ that were not included in the Catholic canon of the New Testament. In the first century and a half of the Christian era, the term *Gnostic* came to denote a section of the early Christian community who professed a belief not simply in Christ and his message but in a revelatory experience of the divine. The Greek word *gnosis* connotes "knowledge" or the "act of knowing." Gnosis is not a rational, propositional, logical understanding but a knowing acquired by experience.

Gnosticism asserts that "direct, personal and absolute knowledge of the authentic truths of existence is accessible to human beings," and that the attainment of such knowledge is the supreme achievement of life. The Gnostics were less interested in dogma or rational theology than in the ongoing force of divine revelation. It is this knowledge, gained from interior comprehension and personal experience, that constitutes gnosis. The first leaders of Gnostic Christianity were teachers in the catechetical school of Alexandria in the early part of the second century.[7]

The Gnostic Basilides was one of the earliest known Christian teachers at Alexandria. Born in the first century CE, he flourished under the emperors Hadrian and Antoninus Pius, about 120–140. Basilides was conversant with the Hebrew Scriptures and Christian Gospels, as well as with ancient Egyptian wisdom. He adapted the idea of Christ to the Gnostic panorama of the universe. According to the church father Irenaeus of Lyons (in *Against the Heretics,* 1.24, written about 170 CE), Basilides taught that *nous* (mind) was the first to be born from the Unborn Father; from *nous* was born *logos* (reason); from *logos, phronēsis* (prudence); from *phronēsis, sophia* (wisdom) and *dunamis* (strength); and from *dunamis* and *sophia,* the Virtues, Principalities, and Archangels. The highest heaven was made by these angelic hosts, their descendants made the second heaven, and their descendants in turn made the third, and so on till they reached the number 365. Hence the year has as many days as there are heavens.

According to Basilides, the angels who hold the last or visible heaven brought about all things that are in the world and shared among themselves the Earth and the nations upon it. The highest of these angels is the one who is thought to be the God of the Old Testament. He wished to make the other nations subject to his people, but the other angelic principalities withstood him to the utmost. The Unborn and Nameless

Father, seeing their miserable plight, sent his firstborn, *nous* (identified with Christ), to deliver those who would believe in him from the power of the angelic agencies. Christ seemed to be a man and to have performed miracles. But it was not Christ who suffered on the cross but Simon of Cyrene. Simon took on Jesus's form and was crucified in his stead. Jesus stood by and laughed at them, then returned to his Father. Through the gnosis of Christ the souls of men are saved, even though their bodies perish.

Clement of Alexandria gives us a few glimpses into the ethical side of Basilides's system in his *Stromata* or *Miscellanies,* written around 210 (1.21; 2.6, 8, 20; 4.11, 12, 25; 5.1, etc.). He tells us that, nominally, faith was the beginning of the spiritual life; it was not, however, a free submission of the intellect but a natural gift of understanding (gnosis) bestowed upon the soul before its union with the body, and which some possessed while others did not. Faith is a latent force that only manifests its energy through the coming of the Savior, as a ray of light will set naphtha on fire. Sin was not the result of the abuse of free will but the outcome of an inborn evil principle.

THE GOSPEL OF TRUTH

Until the discovery of the Nag Hammadi library in 1945, the Gnostic view of early Christianity had largely been forgotten. The teachings of the Gnostics—vilified as heretics by the Catholic church—had been virtually erased from history by the early church fathers; their gospels were banned and even burned to make room for the Christian theology outlined in the canonical Gospels of Matthew, Mark, Luke, and John.

The Nag Hammadi library includes a number of "Gnostic Gospels"—texts once thought to have been entirely destroyed during the early Christian struggle to control orthodoxy, such as *The Gospel of Thomas, The Gospel of Philip,* and *The Gospel of Truth.* Here is an excerpt from *The Gospel of Truth:*

The gospel of truth is joy to those who have received from the Father of truth the gift of knowing him, through the power of the Word that came forth from the pleroma, the one who is in the thought and mind of the Father, that is, the one who is addressed as the Savior, (that) being the name of the work he is to perform for the redemption of those who were ignorant of the Father, while the name [of] the gospel is the proclamation of hope, being discovery for those who search for him.

When the totality went about searching for the one from whom they had come forth—and the totality was inside of him, the incomprehensible, inconceivable one who is superior to every thought. . . .

Through this, the gospel of the one who is searched for, which <was> revealed to those who are perfect through the mercies of the Father, the hidden mystery, Jesus the Christ, enlightened those who were in darkness through oblivion. He enlightened them; he showed (them) a way; and the way is the truth which he taught them. . . .

As for the incomprehensible, inconceivable one, the Father, the perfect one, the one who made the totality, within him is the totality and of him the totality has need. . . .

There was manifested in their heart the living book of the living—the one written in the thought and the mind [of the] Father . . . that (book) which no one was able to take, since it remains for the one who will take it to be slain. . . . For this reason, . . . the faithful one, Jesus, was patient in accepting sufferings until he took that book, since he knows that his death meant life for many. . . . He draws himself down to death though life eternal clothes him. . . .

This <is> the word of the gospel of the discovery of the pleroma, for those who await the salvation which is coming from on high.[8]

By the late fourth century CE, when Christianity became the officially approved religion of the Roman empire, possession of books denounced as heretical was made a criminal offense. Copies of these books were burned and destroyed. But in Upper Egypt, someone took some banned books and hid them in jars, where they remained for about sixteen hundred years.

The documents showed that Gnostic Christianity was not the depraved cult described by the orthodox Christian writers, but rather a legitimate religious movement that offered an alternative testament to Jesus's life and teachings.[9]

GNOSTICISM IN ROME

We have a Roman witness of the Gnostic nature of early Christianity in Alexandria during the first half of the second century. It shows that the Alexandrian Christians, although worshipping Christ, kept their ancient beliefs. In 134 CE, following his visit to Alexandria, the Roman emperor Hadrian wrote a letter to his elderly brother-in-law, the consul Servianus, quoted by Flavius Vopiscus, *Vita Saturini* 8: "So, you praise Egypt, my very dear Servianus! I know the land from top to bottom. . . . In it the worshippers of Serapis are Christians, and those who call themselves Bishops of Christ pay their vows to Serapis."

That Gnosticism was in the mainstream of Christianity in the first two centuries of the Common Era is attested by the fact that one of its most influential teachers, Valentinus, was in consideration during the mid-second century for election as the bishop of Rome. Born in Alexandria around 100 CE, Valentinus distinguished himself at an early age and became an extraordinary teacher and leader in the Alexandrian Christian community. While he regarded Jesus as the Savior, Valentinus believed that man lives in an absurd world that can be rendered meaningful only by gnosis. In his myth of the creation, Valentinus shifts the blame for the defective cosmos from humanity to creative divinity. Irenaeus quotes Valentinus concerning this:

Perfect redemption is the cognition itself of the ineffable greatness: for since through ignorance came about the defect . . . the whole system springing from ignorance is dissolved in Gnosis. Therefore, Gnosis is the redemption of the inner man; and it is not of the body, for the body is corruptible; nor is it psychical, for even the soul is a product of the defect and it is a lodging to the spirit: pneumatic (spiritual) therefore also must be redemption itself. Through Gnosis, then, is redeemed the inner, spiritual man: so that to us suffices the Gnosis of universal being: and this is the true redemption. (*Against the Heresies,* 1.21.4)

While still in his prime, ca. 136–140 CE, Valentinus migrated from Alexandria to Rome and played an important role in the affairs of the church there up to the year 160. He professed to have received a special apostolic sanction through Theudas, a disciple and initiate of Paul. The church father Tertullian wrote that Valentinus was a candidate for the office of bishop of Rome around 140 and that he lost the election by a rather narrow margin. Valentinus, who became a priest in the church and could even have become a bishop, was never condemned as a heretic in his lifetime and remained a respected member of the Christian community until his death.

The situation changed toward the end of the second century, when the church fathers started to define what they regarded as orthodox belief and to establish the ecclesiastical order of the church. By 180 Irenaeus had published his first attacks on Gnosticism as heresy, a work that was continued with increasing vehemence throughout the next century. What became identified as Orthodox Christianity developed as a result of the fathers' attempt to define what is *not* to be regarded as heresy in their confrontation with the Gnostic teachers. By the end of the fourth century the struggle was over: Gnosticism as a Christian tradition was largely eradicated by the force of the Roman state, its remaining teachers ostracized, and its sacred books destroyed.

Freemasons regard Hiram Abiff, rather than Jesus, to be their Savior. Here again, surprisingly enough, they have a point. Where did they get this belief from? It could only be a memory of an ancient tradition that was lost during the Middle Ages. Although Jesus is certainly the Christ, or Messiah, it was the cult of the architect, son of Habu, that created early Christianity.

THE MARGINALIZATION OF EGYPT

When the Romans began to govern, they closed all Egyptian temples, with the exception of the Serapeum of Alexandria, which contained the great library of Alexandria and its precious scrolls of Egyptian knowledge, including Gnostic wisdom. Looking for salvation, the Therapeutae meditated throughout deserted areas, where they would be safe to seek the knowledge of the Spirit. It was the convictions of these people, who held ancient Egyptian beliefs in relation to the five books of Moses, that were translated into Greek in Alexandria and produced the writing of Nag Hammadi, even before Jesus had been introduced as the redeemer, son of God. Although the Gnostic communities, as confirmed by Eusebius, represented the earliest emergence of Christianity in Egypt, the church of Rome refused to accept his account, claiming that Christianity did not spread among the Egyptians before the third or even the fourth century.

How could Rome justify its claim, when it is a well-known fact that the earliest center for Christian studies was not in Rome, Asia Minor, or Syria, but in Alexandria? The catechetical school of Alexandria, the oldest in the world, was teaching Christian theology as early as the second half of the second century, when both Christians and pagans were admitted. The school prepared young clerics for the priesthood, and their studies included philosophy as well as theology. The catechetical school of Alexandria is known to have been the most important institution of religious learning in Christendom, where many prominent bishops from different parts of the world were instructed under scholars such as Athenagoras, Clement, Didymus, and especially Origen, who is considered the father of Christian theology. Many scholars, such as Jerome, visited the school of Alexandria to communicate directly with its scholars.

The German theologian Walter Bauer argued that the silence in the early sources about Egyptian church leadership in the first two centuries was due to the fact that the dominant form of early Christianity in Egypt was of a Gnostic type that was later considered heretical by the Catholic church. Scholar Helmut Koester writes:

> In his book *Orthodoxy and Heresy,* first published in 1934, Walter Bauer provided an answer to the astounding absence of reliable sources [in Christian literature] for the Christian beginnings in Egypt. Seen from the perspective of the later Catholic Church, Bauer argues, the beginnings of Christianity in Egypt were "heretical." And therefore, Christian writings composed in Egypt in the early period were not preserved, while other pieces of information were suppressed or not admitted to the treasure of ecclesiastical tradition.[10]

In modern times, even after the emergence of solid evidence confirming the spread of Christianity in Egypt during this period, some church historians have still insisted on denying the existence of early Egyptian Christianity on the same grounds. Archaeological remains uncovered in Egypt clearly show that Christian communities did exist in the country as early as the start of the second century. Christian scriptures were found in Egypt that later became part of the orthodox canon. "Of the fourteen Christian texts that I would date before CE 200 there is only one, the first fragment of the Gospel of Thomas from Oxyrhynchus, which may be reasonably be regarded as Gnostic."[11]

It is true that the early Christian communities in Egypt were diverse in their teachings, with many who were regarded as Gnostics. But this was not the case in Egypt alone; after all, the Gnostic Valentinus taught in Rome as he had taught in Alexandria. At the time, in the mid-second century, orthodoxy had not yet been defined. "The essence of the argument is that early Egyptian Christianity was Gnostic through and through: that, while there may have been individual Christians who were not Gnostics. . . . This is part of Bauer's general thesis that everywhere and not only in Egypt 'heresy' was primary and 'orthodoxy' secondary."[12]

Irenaeus was the first person to attack the Gnostic teachers as heretics. He wrote a number of books, but the most important is the five-volume *On the Detection and Overthrow of the So-Called Gnosis*, normally referred to as *Adversus Haereses* (*Against Heresies*). Irenaeus wrote this book in Greek ca. 180. Its purpose was to refute the teachings of the various Gnostic groups that existed in the second century, not only in Egypt, but also in Rome and other Christian centers. Until the discovery of the Nag Hammadi library in 1945, *Against Heresies* was one of very few surviving sources that we had for Gnosticism.

From the end of the second century, Gnosticism as a theological doctrine or system was rejected by ecclesiastical authority as false. As the nascent Catholic church considered itself to be the custodian of a divinely imparted revelation, it claimed to be the only source that was authorized to expound doctrine under the inspiration of the Holy Spirit. Any interpretation that differed from its official one was regarded as heretical.

ORTHODOXY

The word *orthodox* means "holding the right or correct opinion." In theology, it indicates a right faith, true belief, or sound opinion, in accordance with what is accepted theological and ecclesiastical doctrine. *Orthodox* later also became the specific epithet applied to the Eastern

Church. The classic view of orthodoxy is that it represents the teaching advocated by Jesus and his apostles; those Christians who deny this teaching are heretics. Heresy, then, represents a diversion from the original teachings of Christianity into ideas drawn from outside, mainly from pagan philosophies, such as that of Hermes Trismegistus.

However, *orthodoxy,* in the sense of a unified group advocating an apostolic doctrine accepted by the majority of Christians everywhere, did not exist in the first three centuries. Early Christianity embodied a number of divergent forms, no one of which represented the clear and powerful majority of believers against the others. Orthodox Christianity became identified as such only as a result of the bishops' attacks on what they regarded as heretical Christianity—that is, Gnosticism. But writers of the second and third centuries, such as Origen, Hippolytus, Tertullian, Irenaeus, and Justin, identified orthodoxy only by rejecting what they regarded as heresy, stressing the notion of the apostolic succession.

In their conflict with the Gnostic teachers, the bishops had to define what they regarded as the true faith. It was no longer enough to be baptized on the confession of the risen Christ to be accepted as a member of the Christian community. In order to keep out those they regarded as heretical, the church fathers introduced the Christian creed from the end of the second century on. It is a fixed formula, summarizing the essential articles they regarded as representing the true faith and embodying the basic beliefs of the church. Whoever confessed the creed, accepted baptism, and obeyed the clergy was accepted as a Christian. Anyone who had different views was regarded as a heretic and expelled from the church.

In the New Testament and the primitive Church documents, however, no creed statement as such exists. During the apostolic period of the first century, there was no set formula for confessing Christian faith. What is called the Apostles' Creed does not go back to apostolic times. The Apostles simply preached salvation through the death and resurrection of Jesus Christ as the Son of God. In Acts, before Philip baptizes the Ethiopian eunuch, the latter declares: "I believe that Jesus Christ is the Son of God" (Acts 8:37). Paul writes, "If you confess with your mouth, 'Jesus is Lord,' and believe in your heart that God raised him from the dead, you will be saved" (Romans 10:9). The main points of belief at this period were mainly the confession that Jesus is the Christ, Son of God, who died and was risen in the third day.

This position began to change, however, when Ignatius of Antioch (ca. 116) made quasi-creedal statements based on the primitive kerygma: "Jesus Christ, who was descended from David, and was also of Mary . . . he was truly persecuted under Pontius Pilate; He was truly crucified, and [truly] died, in the sight of beings in heaven, and on earth."[13]

This was the first time Pontius Pilate was mentioned in regard to Jesus's death, together with his crucifixion. Gnostics were claiming that Christ appeared only in visions to different disciples in different parts of the world at different times. By fixing a date and place and the method of his death and resurrection, the nascent Catholic church tried to deny these claims. Nevertheless, by the beginning of the third century, the Roman creed took its final shape, including mention of the ecclesiastical organization of the church as part of the confession: "I believe in God the Father Almighty; and in Christ Jesus His only Son, our Lord, who was conceived of the Holy Spirit, born of the Virgin Mary, suffered under Pontius Pilate, was crucified, died, and was buried; . . . on the third day he rose again from the dead, he ascended to heaven, and is seated on the right hand of the Father, whence he will come to judge the living and the dead. I believe in the Holy Spirit, the holy Catholic church, the forgiveness of sins, the resurrection of the body, and life everlasting."

ECUMENICAL COUNCILS

Later, the ecumenical church councils became the instrument for defining orthodoxy and condemning heresy. The first attempt to gather a body of bishops representing the whole Christian world was the council called by the emperor Constantine I at Nicaea, in northwestern Asia Minor, in the summer of 325. With the style and procedure of the Roman Senate, the 318 bishops who assembled laid the groundwork for the common creed. The bishops of the whole Christian world were now publicly recognized as the senate of the church. In 381, fifty-six years later, the emperor Theodosius I convoked the second ecumenical council at Constantinople. A letter was issued by the synod in 382, including the text of the creed that was agreed upon, which became the core of all future confessions: "We believe in one God, the Father almighty . . . and in one Lord Jesus Christ the only begotten Son of God . . . who because of our salvation came down from heaven, and was incarnate from the Holy Spirit and the Virgin Mary and became man, and suffered and was buried. and rose again on the third day according to the Scriptures, and ascended to heaven . . . and will come again with glory to judge living and dead . . . who spoke through the prophets; in one holy Catholic and apostolic Church."

The name *catholic church* or *church universal* was first applied to the whole body of believers as distinguished from an individual congregation or a particular body of Christians. In the early second century, Ignatius, bishop of Antioch, was arrested, brought to Rome by armed guards, and eventually martyred there in the arena. In his farewell letter to his fellow Christians in Smyrna (present-day Izmir in modern Turkey), he made the first written mention in history of the Catholic church, writing, "Where the bishop is present, there is the Catholic church" (*To the Smyrnaeans*, 8:2).

From the third century on, the idea of doctrine was superadded, so the term *catholic* came to connote the church as orthodox, in opposition to heretics. By 325, the bishops of the first ecumenical council in Nicaea were legislating in the name of the universal body that they called in the official documents "the Catholic church." At that time five chief Christian communities existed, each headed by a patriarch:

in Rome, Constantinople, Alexandria, Antioch, and Jerusalem. It was that same council that formulated the basic creed in which the term *catholic* was retained as one of the marks of the true church of Christ. From the fifth century on, the idea of the unity of the universal church was added to the term *catholic*. Thus, at least in the Western half of what had been the Roman empire, the church of Rome was able to establish itself as the head of the Catholic church—the one, holy, catholic, and apostolic Church founded by Jesus Christ.

THE TRIUMPH OF CATHOLICISM

When the emperor Constantine I adopted the new faith, Christianity became the officially approved religion of the Roman empire. Constantine also granted political power to the Roman church. The bishops of Rome were recognized as councillors of state and obtained juridical rights. The bishops wasted no time in using their newly acquired power to spread the word of God and stamp out his enemies, who were not only the pagans but also the Gnostics of Egypt. At that point the bishops, using the power of the state, declared the possession of what they regarded as heretical books as a criminal offense and ordered them to be destroyed. That was the time, in the mid-fourth century, when someone in the town of Nag Hammadi in Upper Egypt decided to save the Coptic library by putting it in some jars that he buried on a cliff.

The conflict between Roman Christianity and paganism came to a head with the ascent of the emperor Theodosius I, a zealous defender of Catholic Christianity and a fiery enemy of paganism. He set about on a systematic obliteration of all opposition to the Catholic church, especially in Egypt.

One day in 391, the Catholic bishop Theophilus marched from his headquarters in the Brucheion (royal quarter) of Alexandria at the head of a large, howling mob, heading west for the Serapeum in the heart of the Egyptian quarter of Rhakotis. The Serapeum, which had been the center of Egyptian worship for seven centuries, was adorned with extensive columned halls, statues, and many other works of art, as well as being the house of the great Alexandrian library. The frenzied mob, led by Theophilus, rushed through the street along the Canopic way, turning into the short street that led to the temple area of Serapis and meeting other crowds there, before climbing up the great flight of marble steps.

They jumped across the stone platform and into the temple area, where the events of the final tragedy took place. In their agitation, the angry mob took little heed of the gold and silver ornaments, the precious jewels, the priceless bronze and marble statues, the rare murals and tapestries, the carved and painted pillars of granite and marble, the ebony and scented woods, the ivory and exotic furniture—all were smashed to pieces with cries of pleasure. But that was not all. The shouting men, full of demonic delight, turned to the library under the temple, where hundreds of thousands of papyrus rolls and parchments, inscribed with ancient wisdom and knowledge, were taken off their shelves, torn to pieces, and thrown onto bonfires.

This is how the Hermetic Gnostic teaching, originating with Hiram Abiff, the historical Amenhotep, son of Habu, which had given birth to Christianity, was suppressed and persecuted. But the soul of ancient Egyptian sage Hermes lived on secretly in the hearts and minds of some people, until the mid-sixteenth century, when Marsilio Ficino translated the *Corpus Hermeticum,* reviving the memory of the glorious past.

From Mythology to History

ALTHOUGH THE BIBLE HAS MANY mythological accounts, it also portrays some major characters as real historical persons. It is said that Joseph, the son of Jacob, after being sold as a slave in Egypt, became a minister and a close friend of the pharaoh. These events are said to have taken place during the seventeenth century BCE, when the Hyksos, shepherd kings, ruled Egypt.

The Bible asserts that King David established a great empire, with its borders extending between the Euphrates in northern Syria and the borders of Egypt, during the tenth century BCE. David is also said to have been succeeded on the throne by his son, Solomon, who ruled the empire in peace and built a great Temple in Jerusalem. The Temple was built under the supervision of Hiram, known to the Freemasons as Hiram Abiff.

During the 1400s, a Greek copy of the ancient Egyptian *Corpus Hermeticum* reached the Italian city of Florence and was quickly translated into Latin. This translation caused a great revelation within the Western world, which gave birth to the modern Renaissance.

From these texts the Grand Lodge of Freemasonry was established in England in 1717, and the Masonic central ritual formed around the Temple of Solomon and Hiram Abiff, the legendary Phoenician architect whose name is based upon the biblical account as being responsible for building the Temple. Freemasons associated Hiram Abiff with Hermes

Trismegistus, whom they regarded as the first teacher of wisdom and magic and whose teaching eventually produced the Gnostic philosophy.

In modern times, however, historians and archaeologists have completely failed to find any evidence to confirm the biblical accounts of these characters or of the existence of Hiram Abiff in Phoenicia or his Temple in Jerusalem. As a result, many serious historians have concluded that the kingdom of David and Solomon never existed.

However, when we set aside biblical chronology and start looking for historical evidence, we do find confirmation of the Bible stories, only in different times and different locations. When we look in history for an empire that extended between the Euphrates and Egypt, we do find it—exactly as the Bible describes it—not during the time of David in the tenth century BCE, but during the reign of Tuthmosis III in the fifteenth century BCE. We come to the same conclusion with the king of peace who inherited the empire: again, we find him living in Egypt during the fourteenth century BCE, and known as Amenhotep III. In these new dates we can find evidence of the biblical account in all its details.

When we realize that it was Pharaoh Tuthmosis III, not Abraham the Hebrew, who fathered Isaac, the ancestor of Israel, the biblical story moves from the realm of mythology to become part of history. Here we can see how, when the descendants of the two branches of Pharaoh Tuthmosis III were united, a new age of magic, wisdom, and knowledge was born. For while Sarah the Hebrew brought him the line of Isaac, Jacob, and David, Satiah, his queen, brought him the line of Amenhotep II, Tuthmosis IV, and Amenhotep III. When Amenhotep III married Tiye the daughter of Joseph (Yuya) and made her his queen, the two branches of the pharaoh's descendants were united. Then, over a span of 150 years, they produced the first monotheistic belief system as well as philosophical teachings that we have to this day. It was during this short time that the historical background of the Bible stories, as well as the Hermetic philosophy later associated with Hermes Trismegistus and his magic, came to be.

Notes

CHAPTER 2.
THE TWO DAVIDS

1. Garsiel, "The Book of Samuel," 7.
2. Garsiel, "The Book of Samuel," 23.
3. Keys, "Leading Archaeologist Says Old Testament Stories Are Fiction."
4. Davies, "'House of David' Built on Sand," 55.

CHAPTER 3.
THE EVIDENCE OF ARCHAEOLOGY

1. Pritchard, ed., *Ancient Near Eastern Texts,* 262.
2. Gardiner, *Egypt of the Pharaohs,* 285.
3. Kenyon, *The Bible and Recent Archaeology,* 63.
4. Finkelstein and Silberman, *David and Solomon,* 269.
5. Davies, *The History of Ancient Israel,* 117.
6. Draper, "Kings of Controversy."
7. Draper, "Kings of Controversy."
8. Davies, *The History of Ancient Israel,* 116.
9. Osman, *The House of the Messiah,* 120.
10. Davies, *The History of Ancient Israel,* 113.

CHAPTER 4. DAVID'S EMPIRE

1. Quoted in Gardiner, *Egypt of the Pharaohs,* 190.
2. Quoted in Gardiner, *Egypt of the Pharaohs,* 190.
3. Quoted in Pritchard, *Ancient Near Eastern Texts,* 236–37.

4. Pritchard, *Ancient Near Eastern Texts*, 237.

5. Quoted in Gardiner, *Egypt of the Pharaohs*, 194.

CHAPTER 5. THE CHOSEN ONE

1. Breasted, *Ancient Records of Egypt*, 60–61.

2. Maspero, *The Struggle of the Nations*, 289.

3. Maspero, *The Struggle of the Nations*, 289.

4. Hayes, *The Scepter of Egypt*, 116–17.

5. Roth, ed., *Encyclopaedia Judaica*, 7:757.

CHAPTER 6.
SARAH AND THE PHARAOH

1. Baskin, *Midrashic Women*, 138.

2. Eerdmans, "The Hebrews in Egypt," 193–207.

CHAPTER 7.
JERUSALEM, CITY OF DAVID

1. Pritchard, *Ancient Near Eastern Texts*, 236.

CHAPTER 8.
DAVID AND BATHSHEBA

1. Gray, *A History of Jerusalem*, 67.

CHAPTER 9. GOLIATH THE GIANT

1. The translation of the autobiography of Sinuhe here is based on the work of Gardiner, *Note on the Story of Sinuhe,* as well as Simpson, ed., *The Literature of Ancient Egypt.*

2. Pritchard, *The Times Atlas of the Bible*, 32.

3. Simpson, ed., *The Literature of Ancient Egypt*, 64.

CHAPTER 10. JOSEPH'S DREAMS

1. Polano, *Selections from the Talmud*, 83–84. Emphasis in original.

CHAPTER 11.
THE DREAMER PHARAOH

1. Bronner, *From Eve to Esther*, 138.

2. Sayce, ed., *Records of the Past*, 56.

CHAPTER 12.
UNITING THE FAMILIES OF EGYPT AND CANAAN

1. Breasted, *Ancient Records of Egypt*, 2:344–45.
2. Breasted, *Ancient Records of Egypt*, 3:349.
3. Weigall, *The Life and Times of Akhnaton*.
4. Moran, *The Amarna Letters*, and Mercer, ed., *The Tell El-Amarna Tablets*.

CHAPTER 13.
THE EMPIRE OF THE KING OF PEACE

1. Stephen and Boardman, eds., *The Cambridge Ancient History*.
2. Giles, *Ikhnaton*, 159.
3. Conder, *The Tell Amarna Tablets*, 2.
4. Ash, *David, Solomon, and Egypt*, 114.
5. Moran, *The Amarna Letters*, 317.
6. Lichtheim, *Ancient Egyptian Literature*, vol. 2.
7. Pritchard, *Ancient Near Eastern Texts*, 262.
8. Kenyon, *The Bible and Recent Archaeology*, 63.
9. Lipinski, *On the Skirts of Canaan in the Iron Age*, 96–97.
10. O'Connor and Chine, eds., *Amenhotep III*, 92.
11. Otto Eissfeldt, in Stephen and Boardman, eds., *The Cambridge Ancient History*, 2:597.
12. Bright, *A History of Israel*, 205.

CHAPTER 14.
THE "LOST" MINES OF SOLOMON

1. Rothenberg, *Timna*, 9–10.
2. Rothenberg, ed., *The Ancient Metallurgy of Copper*, xv.
3. Rothenberg, *Timna*, 17, 19, 22.
4. Carroll, "King Solomon's Mines Rediscovered?"

CHAPTER 15. WISDOM AND MAGIC

1. Verheyden, *The Figures of Solomon*, 110–11.
2. Ebeling, *Secret History*, 28.
3. Ebeling, *Secret History*, 47.
4. *The Testament of Truth*, 69–70, in Robinson, ed., *The Nag Hammadi Library*, 458. Emphasis added.
5. Ebeling, *Secret History*, 47, 48.

6. Ebeling, *Secret History,* 49.

7. Horstmanshoff and Stol, *Magic and Rationality,* 123–24.

CHAPTER 16. THE LOST PALACE

1. Hayes, "Inscriptions from the Palace of Amenhotep III."

2. Badawy, *A History of Egyptian Architecture.*

3. Milstein, "King Solomon's Wall Found."

4. Seidel, "Archaeologists Link Remains of Destroyed Palace to Reign of King Solomon."

5. Patch, "The Joint Expedition to Malqata, the Palace-City of Amenhotep III."

CHAPTER 17.
THE TEMPLES OF SOLOMON AND AMENHOTEP III

1. Horne, *King Solomon's Temple,* 197.

2. Horne, *King Solomon's Temple,* 203.

3. Albright, *The Archaeology of Palestine,* 123–24.

4. Garstang, *The Heritage of Solomon.*

5. Adams, *Ancient Records and the Bible,* 297.

6. Horne, *King Solomon's Temple,* 64–65.

7. Garber, quoted in Albright, *The Archaeology of Palestine,* 154.

8. Curtis, ed., *The London Encyclopaedia or Universal Dictionary,* vol.2, 589.

9. Redford, *Akhenaten.*

10. Breasted, *Ancient Records of Egypt,* 355–59.

11. Katzenstein, *The History of Tyre,* 78.

12. Feldman, *Josephus in Modern Scholarship (1937–1980),* 174.

13. Katzenstein, *The History of Tyre,* 29.

14. Moran, *The Amarna Letters,* 233.

CHAPTER 18. SECRETS OF THE ARCHITECT

1. Mackey, *Encyclopedia of Freemasonry,* 4.

2. Pirtle, *A Kentucky Monitor,* 14, 15.

3. Breasted, *Ancient Records of Egypt,* 219.

4. Wildung, *Egyptian Saints,* 105.

5. Wildung, *Egyptian Saints,* 105.

6. Josephus, *Against Apion,* 259.

7. Josephus, *Against Apion,* 277.

8. Josephus, *Against Apion,* 269.

9. Quoted in Bradley, *Ancient Egypt.*

10. Quoted in Morenz, *Egyptian Religion,* 102.

11. Wildung, *Egyptian Saints,* 195.

12. Steindorff and Seele, *When Egypt Ruled the East,* 77.

13. Teeter, *Religion and Ritual in Ancient Egypt,* 100.

14. Ockinga, "Amenhotep, Son of Hapu."

15. Lichtheim, *Ancient Egyptian Literature,* vol. 3, 104.

16. Wildung, *Egyptian Saints,* 105.

17. Yates, *The Occult Philosophy in the Elizabethan Age.*

18. Assmann, foreword to Ebeling, *Secret History.*

19. In Robinson, *The Nag Hammadi Library,* 321–27. The text refers to itself as *The Eighth Reveals the Ninth,* 326.

20. Price, *Angels within Us,* 40–41.

21. Horstmanshoff and Stol, *Magic and Rationality,* 139.

CHAPTER 19.
THE BIRTH AND REPRESSION OF GNOSTICISM

1. Philo Judaeus, translated by Tilden, *On the Contemplative Life,* 7, 8.

2. Philo Judaeus, translated by Tilden, *On the Contemplative Life,* 12.

3. Philo Judaeus, translated by Tilden, *On the Contemplative Life,* 10.

4. Philo Judaeus, translated by Tilden, *On the Contemplative Life,* 8.

5. Chadwick, *A Study in Primitive Monasticism,* 14.

6. de Vlieger, *The Coptic Church,* 18.

7. Roberts, *Manuscript, Society, and Belief,* 54.

8. *The Gospel of Truth,* 16 –20, 34; in Robinson, *The Nag Hammadi Library,* 40–42, 47. All parentheses and square and angled bracketed insertions are in the original.

9. Grant, *Gnosticism,* in Barnstone, *The Other Bible.*

10. Koester, *History and Literature of Early Christianity,* 227.

11. Roberts, *Manuscript, Society, and Belief,* 51.

12. Roberts, *Manuscript, Society, and Belief,* 49–50.

13. Saint Ignatius, translated by Schaff, *The Sacred Writings of Ignatius,* Epistle to the Trallians.

Bibliography

Adams, J. Mckee. *Ancient Records and the Bible.* Nashville: Broadman Press, 1946.

Albright, William Foxwell. *The Archaeology of Palestine.* London: Penguin Books, 1949.

Ash, Paul S. *David, Solomon, and Egypt: A Reassessment.* London: A & C Black, 1999.

Badawy, Alexander. *A History of Egyptian Architecture.* Berkeley: University of California Press, 1968.

Barnstone, Willis. *The Other Bible.* San Francisco: Harper & Row, 1984.

Baskin, Judith R. *Midrashic Women.* Waltham, MA: Brandeis University, 2002.

Bradley, Pamela. *Ancient Egypt: Reconstructing the Past.* Cambridge: Cambridge University Press, 1999.

Breasted, John Henry. *Ancient Records of Egypt,* volumes 2 and 3. Champaign: University of Illinois Press, 2001. Originally published in 1906.

Bright, John. *A History of Israel.* Louisville, KY: Westminster John Knox Press, 1981.

Bronner, Leila Leah. *From Eve to Esther.* Louisville, KY: Westminster John Knox Press, 1994.

Carroll, Rebecca. "King Solomon's Mines Rediscovered?" *National Geographic.* October 28, 2008.

Chadwick, Owen. *A Study in Primitive Monasticism.* Cambridge: University of Cambridge Press, 1950.

Conder, Claude Reignier. *The Tell Amarna Tablets.* Ulan Press, 2012. The book was originally published prior to 1923.

Curtis, Thomas, ed. *The London Encyclopaedia or Universal Dictionary,* volume 2. London: Thomas Tegg, 1834.

Davies, Philip R. *The History of Ancient Israel.* London: Bloomsbury, 2015.

———. "'House of David' Built on Sand: The Sins of the Biblical Maximizers." *Biblical Archaeology Review* 20, no. 4 (July–August, 1994).

de Vlieger, Rev. A. *The Coptic Church.* Lausanne, Switzerland: George Bridel, 1900.

Draper, Robert. "Kings of Controversy." *National Geographic.* December 2010.

Ebeling, Florian. *The Secret History of Hermes Trismegistus.* Foreword by Jan Assmann. Translated by David Lorton. Ithaca, NY: Cornell University Press, 2007.

Eerdmans, B. D. "The Hebrews in Egypt." *Expositor.* September 1908.

Feldman, Louis H. *Josephus in Modern Scholarship (1937–1980).* Berlin: De Gruyter, 1984.

Finkelstein, Israel, and Neil Asher Silberman. *David and Solomon: In Search of the Bible's Sacred Kings and the Roots of the Western Tradition.* New York: Free Press, 2006.

Gardiner, Alan H. *Egypt of the Pharaohs.* Oxford: Oxford University Press, 1966.

———. *Note on the Story of Sinuhe.* CreateSpace, 2014.

Garsiel, Moshe. "The Book of Samuel: Its Composition, Structure, and Significance." *Journal of Hebrew Scriptures* 10, article 5 (2009).

Garstang, John. *The Heritage of Solomon.* London: Institute of Archaeology, University of Liverpool, 1934.

Giles, Frederick J. *Ikhnaton: Legend and History.* Madison, NJ: Fairleigh Dicknson University Press, 1972.

Grant, Robert M. *Gnosticism.* New York: Harper & Brothers, 1961.

Gray, John. *A History of Jerusalem.* London: Robert Hale, 1969.

Hayes, William C. "Inscriptions from the Palace of Amenhotep III." *Journal of Near Eastern Studies* 10 (1951).

———. *The Scepter of Egypt: A Background for the Study of the Egyptian Antiquities in the Metropolitan Museum of Art, Part 2: The Hyksos Period and the New Kingdom, 1675–1080 BC.* New York: Harry N. Abrams, 1990.

Horne, Alex. *King Solomon's Temple in the Masonic Tradition.* London: Aquarian Press, 1971.

Horstmanshoff, Manfred, and Marten Stol. *Magic and Rationality in Ancient Near Eastern and Greco-Roman Medicine.* Leiden, Netherlands: Brill, 2004.

Josephus, Flavius. *Against Apion*. Translated by H. St. Thackeray. London: Heinmann, 1926.

Judaeus, Philo. *On the Contemplative Life*. Translated by Frank William Tilden. Bloomington, IN: Indiana University Press, 1823.

Katzenstein, Jacob H. *The History of Tyre*. Jerusalem: Schocken Institute for Jewish Research, 1973.

Kenyon, Kathleen M. *The Bible and Recent Archaeology*. Louisville, KY: Westminster John Knox Press, 1978.

Keys, David. "Leading Archaeologist Says Old Testament Stories Are Fiction." *The Independent Newspaper* (London). March 28, 1993.

Koester, Helmut. *History and Literature of Early Christianity*. New York: De Gruyter, 1982.

Lichtheim, Miriam. *Ancient Egyptian Literature: A Book of Readings*. Volume 2: *The New Kingdom*. Berkeley: University of California Press, 1976.

———. *Ancient Egyptian Literature: A Book of Readings*. Volume 3: *The Late Period*. Berkeley: University of California Press, 1980.

Lipinski, Edward. *On the Skirts of Canaan in the Iron Age*. Leuven, Belgium: Peeters, 2006.

Mackey, Albert G. *Encyclopedia of Freemasonry*. Philadelphia: McClure, 1884.

Maspero, Gaston. *The Struggle of the Nations: Egypt, Syria, and Assyria*. Edited by Archibald Henry Sayce. Translated by M. L. McClure. Whitefish, MT: Kessinger, 2010. Originally published in 1896.

Mercer, Samuel A. B., ed. *The Tell El-Amarna Tablets*. London: Macmillan, 1939.

Milstein, Mati. "King Solomon's Wall Found—Proof of Bible Tale?" *National Geographic*. February 27, 2010.

Moran, William L. *The Amarna Letters*. Baltimore, MD: Johns Hopkins University Press, 1992.

Morenz, Siegfried. *Egyptian Religion*. Ithaca, NY: Cornell University Press, 1992.

Ockinga, Boyo. "Amenhotep, Son of Hapu." The Rundle Foundation for Egyptian Archaeology Newsletter, no. 18 (February 1986).

O'Connor, David, and Eric H. Chine, eds., *Amenhotep III: Perspectives on His Reign*. Ann Arbor: University of Michigan Press, 2001.

Osman, Ahmed. *The House of the Messiah*. London: Harper Collins, 1992.

Patch, Diana Craig. "The Joint Expedition to Malqata, the Palace-City of Amenhotep III." ARCE website archives. Northern California Chapter, ARCE (American Research Center in Egypt). Accessed October 17, 2018.

Pirtle, Henry. *A Kentucky Monitor: Complete Monitorial Ceremonies of the Blue Lodge*. Hannibal, MO: Grand Lodge of Kentucky Free and Accepted Masons, 1979.

Polano, H. *Selections from the Talmud*. London: Frederick Warne, 1894.

Price, John Randolph. *Angels within Us*. New York: Random House, 1993.

Pritchard, James B., ed. *Ancient Near Eastern Texts*. Princeton: Princeton University Press, 1955.

———. *The Times Atlas of the Bible*. London: Times Books, 1987.

Redford, Donald B. *Akhenaten: The Heretic King*. Princeton, NJ: Princeton University Press, 1987.

Roberts, Colin H. *Manuscript, Society, and Belief in Early Christian Egypt (The Schweich Lectures of the British Academy, 1977)*. Oxford: Oxford University Press, 1979.

Robinson, James M., ed. *The Nag Hammadi Library*. 3rd ed. San Francisco: HarperSanFrancisco, 1990.

Roth, Cecil, ed. *Encyclopaedia Judaica*. Jerusalem: Keter Publishing House, 1972.

Rothenberg, Beno. *Timna: Valley of the Biblical Copper Mines*. London: Thames and Hudson, 1971.

Rothenberg, Beno, ed. *The Ancient Metallurgy of Copper*. London: Institute of Archaeology/Institute of Archaeo-Metallurgical Studies, 1990.

Saint Ignatius. *The Sacred Writings of Ignatius*. Translated by Philip Schaff. Altenmünster, Germany: Jazzybee Verlag, 2012.

Sayce, Archibald Henry, ed. *Records of the Past*. London: Samuel Bagster and Sons, 1888.

Seidel, Jamie. "Archaeologists Link Remains of Destroyed Palace to Reign of King Solomon." News Corp Australia. September 1, 2016.

Simpson, William Kelly, ed. *The Literature of Ancient Egypt*. New Haven, CT: Yale University Press, 1973.

Steindorff, George, and Keith C. Seele. *When Egypt Ruled the East*. Chicago: University of Chicago Press, 1975.

Stephen, Iowerth Eiddon, and John Boardman, eds. *The Cambridge Ancient History*. Cambridge: Cambridge University Press, 1975.

Stern, Ephraim. *Encyclopaedia of Archaeological Excavations in the Holy Lands*. Edited by Michael Avi-Yonah. Oxford: Oxford University Press, 1978.

Teeter, Emily. *Religion and Ritual in Ancient Egypt*. Cambridge: Cambridge University Press, 2011.

Thomas, D. Winton, ed. *Documents from Old Testament Times*. New York: Harper Collins, 1965.

Verheyden, Joseph. *The Figures of Solomon in Jewish, Christian, and Islamic Tradition*. Leiden, Belgium: Brill, 2012.

Weigall, Arthur. *The Life and Times of Akhnaton*. London: Thornton Butterworth, 1910.

Wildung, Dietrich. *Egyptian Saints: Deification in Pharaonic Egypt*. New York: New York University Press, 1977.

Yates, Frances. *The Occult Philosophy in the Elizabethan Age*. New York: Routledge, 2001.

Index

Page numbers in *italics* indicate illustrations.